Secrets of Successful Selling

Secrets of Successful Selling

Charles R. Whitlock

CB

CONTEMPORARY
BOOKS

CHICAGO

Library of Congress Cataloging-in-Publication Data

Whitlock, Charles R.
    Secrets of successful selling / Charles R. Whitlock.
       p.   cm.
    Includes index.
    ISBN 0-8092-3946-9 (cloth)
       0-8092-3813-6 (paper)
    1. Selling.   I. Title.
HF5438.25.W5   1992
658.8'5—dc20

                            91-44269
                                CIP

Published by Contemporary Books, Inc.
180 North Michigan Avenue, Chicago, Illinois 60601
Manufactured in the United States of America
International Standard Book Number: 0-8092-3946-9 (cloth)
                                     0-8092-3813-6 (paper)

Contents

Acknowledgments

Thanks to the many businesses who sponsor my seminars. A special thanks to Candace Smoral for her editorial assistance and long hours with the reference books. Thanks to Caroline Hotchkiss who spent lots of time typing my manuscript on her favorite computer. Mary Hartig unearthed a lot of terrific information for me. John Helmuth and Tony Giaimo did a great job with the personality-assessment charts. To all of you I am forever grateful.

Thanks to George Wieser and Olga Wieser, my hardworking agents in New York, for their encouragement. A special thanks to Harvey Plotnick, my publisher, and his devoted and ever-helpful staff.

Last, but certainly not least, thanks to all of the thousands of people who have attended my seminars and who will read this book.

1
Introduction

One salesperson sells ten new computers to every one his associates sell. Every year he receives the largest bonus check. His earnings are ten times greater than the earnings of the other salespeople who have attended the same training programs. They see the same number of prospects. In many instances, they come from similar backgrounds. Can one salesperson be lucky year after year? I think not.

I think that the one extremely successful salesperson uncovered the real secret to sales success. He did not make a deal with the devil to trade his soul for financial freedom and the accolades that come from being the best in his field. He did not hypnotize each potential customer into buying a new computer. He did not kidnap the prospect's firstborn and refuse to return the child until a new computer was purchased. He did not put a gun to a prospect's head before asking for a signature on the sales agreement. He *did* use a sales tool that is as powerful and as persuasive as any of these convincing measures. His methods are legal, and his customers keep coming back every time they need new software or another new computer.

WHAT'S THE SECRET?

The secret to what sets this supersalesperson apart from his contemporaries is in this book. For the past twenty-

1

plus years, I have sold considerably more than my fellow sales professionals and competitors. I have been awarded every bonus and almost every prize, and I have earned millions of dollars in sales commissions.

On March 3, 1985, at approximately 10:22 P.M., I died at Westlake Medical Center. Had the cardiologists not brought me back to life with the injection of an anticlotting drug known as streptokinase, my closed arteries would have opened the door to the next world. As I lay there moving in and out of life, all I could think about was how I had lifted myself out of a near-poverty-level existence in Chicago. As a child being raised by a single parent, I never dreamed I'd be living in a multimillion-dollar mansion in an upper-class northern suburb of Los Angeles. I had a new Mercedes every year; the mansion on the hill; the yacht in a nearby slip; the summer home; monthlong ski trips to St. Moritz, Switzerland; chauffeur-driven limousines; and every material thing a person could want. Having learned the real secret to sales success, I was dying and taking the secret to my grave. I felt like someone who had buried an incredible treasure, and only I knew its location.

Fortunately, the following morning on March 4, 1985, at 7:37 A.M., the surgeons removed some veins from my left leg and sutured them around my clogged coronary arteries, and I lived. I now can share my secret with you.

REAL-LIFE SALES STRATEGIES

There are as many books on sales as there are theories of how to sell. When I first launched my career in sales, I read two or three basic sales books that gave me the fundamental information I needed to get started in sales. The books did not prepare me for the rejections, the countless interruptions during presentations, customers who forgot about appointments, government purchasing agents who went out for public open bid after I spent hours educating them on my product, or customers who took payoffs under the table from competitors. Certainly, no book prepared me for employers who reduced my territory as soon as I started to make too much money.

In addition to the basic sales techniques, I am going to discuss the *real-world* aspects of selling. You'll learn how to make effective presentations, handle objections, and probe effectively. I'll address the most powerful closing systems, marketing, the competitive climate, networking, and synergistic sales campaigns. I'll relate real-life sales strategies that helped me close multimillion-dollar deals. How can you qualify your prospect and decrease your prospecting time? How do you overcome obstacles and deal with the customer's idiosyncrasies? Are you effectively using your computer to help you close sales? As a veteran salesperson, I believe this hands-on sales book is essential for anyone who wants to be part of a great industry, who wants to make a great deal of income, and who would like to enjoy the psychological rewards that come from providing an essential service for American business.

I hope you enjoy the personality assessment in Chapter 4. It will give you some valuable insight about yourself. Knowing your own personality will assist you in gaining the greatest understanding about why people behave as they do and why you do things the way you do.

I will share with you some of the sales techniques taught at the world-famous Kanrisha Yosei Gakko training school that was featured on CBS's "60 Minutes." Many of the students who start this world-famous sales school fail. I will share with you my personal opinions about the time I spent at Kanrisha Yosei Gakko.

Without a basic understanding of elemental concepts, it is almost impossible to comprehend higher concepts and techniques that can change our lives. You would have a difficult time working with algebraic equations without having a basic understanding of fundamental mathematics.

Likewise, the secret to being the most successful salesperson in the world cannot be understood without a solid comprehension of the basic sales elements. Read each chapter carefully and complete each assignment. Make certain that you understand the sales processes and techniques described in each chapter before going on to the next. Try not to jump around from chapter to chapter; each chapter builds on the previous one and should be read sequentially. If you have a sales presentation to give tomorrow, you may be tempted to read the chapter on sales presentations first. Resist the temptation at all costs.

You should immediately integrate the techniques discussed in the following chapters—like matching personalities with appropriate closing systems—into your selling style. Keep using them until they become as automatic as knee-jerk reactions. Like most things in life, repetition and reinforcement will be the keys to successfully incorporating these techniques into your daily life.

Don't forget to tell your friends and business associates about my book. (I am jumping the gun, I know. I am supposed to cover networking in another chapter. It's hard for a salesperson not to apply his skills!) If you like this book, use the new insights you've gained and enjoy the increased income that surely will follow. A time-management hint: Carry this book in your briefcase so you can read it while waiting to see your customers.

WHAT DO THE SUCCESSFUL SALESPEOPLE KNOW?

According to Aristotle Onassis, "The secret of business is to know something that nobody else knows." Can you keep a secret? Then read on.

- *Jack Havey* sold $3 million worth of services the past year. A great illustrator and cartoonist, he is also a great salesman. He owns Ad-Media Inc., an advertising agency in Augusta, Maine.
- *Jack Barnett* of Williamsburg, Virginia, sold $5 million worth of candles and soaps the past year.
- *Mary McKenzie* sold nearly $20 million worth of ham, sausage, and hot dogs the past year. A law-school graduate, her business is based in Burlington, Vermont.
- *Korry Hatzes* sold nearly $2 million worth of tablecloth and napkin rentals. Korry and her husband, Bob, operate their business from Silver Spring, Maryland.
- *Rick Corman* sold $2 million worth of railroad-car rentals from his operation in Nicholasville, Kentucky.
- *Jim Berluti* of Boston, Massachusetts, sold $17 million worth of overnight-delivery services.
- *Mike Smith* made his first million dollars this year by selling his weather-reporting service to twenty-nine major newspapers, utility companies, and railroads nationwide. His firm is based in Wichita, Kansas.
- *George Matteson* of Independence, Missouri, sold $8 million worth of imprinted playing cards the past year. His customers include Caesar's Palace and three of the Mississippi River gambling boats.
- *Don Helbling* sold nearly $3 million worth of branding irons to ranchers and farmers throughout the United States, Canada, and Australia from his Mandan, North Dakota, operation.
- *Jim Helzer* sold $33 million worth of collectors' stamps, limited-edition prints, and other collectibles throughout North America. Jim resides in Cheyenne, Wyoming.
- *Bill Mullin, Jr.*, sold nearly $3 million worth of fast foods this year. Now residing in Auburn, California,

Bill started his sales career right after graduating from Colorado State University. He wrote his M.B.A. thesis on the fast-food business.

• *Jeannie Graves* sold $6 million worth of temporary claims and adjusting services. An Irvine, California, resident, Jeannie received her basic sales training at the Aames Bureau of Employment when she worked there.

• *Sheila Cluff* sold $7 million worth of health and fitness services the past year. Sheila started her own health-and-fitness television show and is a superb networker. She resides in Ojai, California.

Each salesperson in this list has shown that he or she has what it takes to become one of the most successful salespeople in the world.

There are 1.2 billion households in the world. These households need furnishings, appliances, bedding, lawn products, construction materials, television sets, radios, stereos, cutlery, wall decorations, Christmas trees, exercise equipment, and doghouses. There are 5 billion people in the world who need food, toiletries, clothing, transportation, education, and recreation. There are 1.8 billion working people who need computers, specialized training, tools, equipment, uniforms, office buildings, office furnishings, interpreters, accountants, lawyers, and architects. There are 1.5 billion children under fifteen in the world who need everything from gym shoes, diapers, toys, scouting uniforms, school supplies, driver's training, drug-abuse education, vaccinations, dental care, and eye care to summer camps, baseball bats, athletic equipment, jeans, watches, and compact discs. These children are taught by 32 million teachers who need textbooks, work manuals, training materials, and higher education. The world's 4 million doctors need medicine, diagnostic instruments, medical equipment, offices, hospitals, ambulances, helicopters, and 32 million nurses.

Did you know that 8,240 daily newspapers report on the world's happenings every day? (It sounds like Mike Smith has a lot of room to grow with his weather-reporting business in Wichita, Kansas.) These newspapers need stories, wire services, art supplies, advertisers, typesetting equipment, printing presses, and trucks. The 527 million television sets must be replaced every 3.9 years and repaired by one of the 2 million television-repair people who needs test equipment, tools, spare parts, specialized training, trucks, and telephones. If you have a telephone, you have one of 453 million telephones in the world that requires trunk lines, carrier systems, switching equipment, reams of paperwork, and, of course, service trucks. If the telephone company has a truck, it is one of 300 million vehicles in the world that, of course, needs wheels, steering wheels, hubcaps, hoses, upholstery, steel, glass, radios and tape decks, and paint. Trucks run on roads that need asphalt, paint, cement, roadside signs, and traffic lights. The top salespeople are going to earn a lot of commissions, overrides, bonuses, and big salaries. This book is dedicated to giving you the tools you need to be one of these people.

2
Sales: A Commonsense Career Choice

"Nothing is really work unless you would rather be doing something else."

—James M. Barrie

Sales is the lifeline to every business in a free democratic society. Without sales, industry does not exist. In its annual issue on selling, *Success* magazine (May 1991) reports a statement by Dr. Thomas J. Stanley, marketing professor at Georgia State University, Atlanta, that more sales and marketing professionals than physicians earn six-figure incomes.

Unlike physicians, accountants, lawyers, and certain other professionals, salespeople are seldom defendants in lawsuits. Comparatively speaking, they incur little risk. Business owners are faced with disgruntled employees, unhappy shareholders, and myriad other risk factors that can have an adverse impact on their incomes. The salesperson, however, develops relationships that, in many cases, enable him to take his accounts wherever he goes. He is cherished by his employer and more often than not is practically indispensable because of his customer relationships. In *Mary Kay on People Management* (Warner

Books, New York), Mary Kay Ash (whose own background is sales) states that she is 100 percent committed to the sales team. "Not a single major decision is ever made at Mary Kay Cosmetics without first weighing the consequences to our sales force." Her belief is that the entire company should be oriented around *sales*.

UNLIMITED GROWTH POTENTIAL

Sales offers a career without financial limitations or geographic boundaries but with unlimited personal growth potential. There is a story that aptly illustrates this idea, the story of the shoe company that sent its best, most experienced salesman to India to open up a new sales office. A week after the salesman arrived in New Delhi, he called the home office and told the vice president of sales that he was coming home because the people of India did not wear shoes, and, therefore, the market potential was pretty dismal. Disappointed but relieved that he had assessed the situation early in the game, he returned to the United States. At a shoe convention, a competitive shoe company heard about this experience and sent its number-one salesman to India to open a sales office. A week after his arrival in New Delhi, he called the home office and asked them to triple the initial shoe inventory because he found unlimited market potential: a whole country in need of shoes.

During my career as a salesman, I have traveled around the world many times. I have visited almost every major city in Europe, Asia, and North America. Years of six-figure incomes were interrupted only by years of seven-figure incomes. I have found sales to be challenging, replete with diversity, and emotionally satisfying. The friendships that developed over the years have given me a rich, full, extraordinary life.

I know of no other career that offers so much to so many.

A career in sales can attract Harvard attorneys, MIT engineers, UCLA physicians, those with no formal education, and everyone in between. Whether you are a student, or a homemaker involved in multilevel marketing to supplement the family income, or a full-time jet aircraft salesman, you will be employing many of the same fundamental techniques. How well you apply those techniques will determine how much money you will earn.

THE ROAD TO SUCCESS

Andrew Carnegie believed that "the true road to preeminent success in any line is to make yourself master of that line." No matter what you ultimately do in life, the sales tools you acquire along the way will help you achieve your goals.

Whether they realize it or not, everyone sells something every day. A mastery of basic communication skills is critical to success in almost any endeavor. Your power of persuasion will help you present your point of view convincingly, and people will respond accordingly. Your ability to assess personality styles will help you in your personal and professional relationships and enable you to attain a level of communication that many people never will achieve even with their loved ones. Once you understand the theory of selling based on a hierarchy of needs, you will be able to deal more effectively with people in all walks of life.

Some of our most dynamic political and industrial leaders began their careers in sales. Lee Iacocca liked working with people more than machines, so after completing an engineering training program at Ford, Iacocca was hired for a low-level desk job in fleet sales. Country music superstar Willie Nelson sold encyclopedias door-to-door when he was trying to get his music career off the ground. Ed McMahon began his illustrious career in sales by selling newspapers and pineapple juice as a child. Later on, he sold passersby Morris Metric Slicers on the Atlantic City boardwalk. James Cash Penney bought and sold pigs as a youngster.

At the age of seventeen, Richard Warren Sears became his family's breadwinner. By selling gold-filled pocket watches to rural customers, he entered into the powerful world of sales. It was reported only a few years later that he could "sell a breath of air." Estēe Lauder honed her sales techniques as a young woman in her father's hardware store. Ray Kroc of McDonald's fame sold paper cups for Lily Tulip Cup Company for seventeen years. While selling a $150 milk-shake machine called a Multimixer, he came upon the San Bernardino, California, McDonald brothers' restaurant. How much of the success of these people can be attributed to their sales experiences? I firmly believe a great deal.

Congratulations on your decision to take this rewarding career path! In what other career can you travel, enjoy unlimited earnings potential, work in an environment that enables you to use your creative and problem-solving abilities, incur little liability, enjoy the freedom to work as hard as your financial needs dictate, make lifelong friendships, and receive accolades from members of your management and associates alike in addition to the psychological rewards of providing solutions to your customers' problems?

No matter what your position on a football team, every touchdown reflects the *team*'s capability. In sales, *you* get to make as many touchdowns as you want. While your corporate teammates may need approval for most of the programs they want to initiate, as a salesperson, you may design the strategy and initiate the program single-handedly in most cases. Being a salesperson quite simply means having the freedom to be all that you can be.

3
The Cream of the Sales Crop

"Success is a matter of luck. Ask any failure."
                                        —Earl Wilson

You probably won't be able to pick out the supersalespeople in a photograph or in a restaurant. Each one has a unique personality and personal style. So what do the most successful salespeople have in common? Plenty!

Because every company has its own products and services, its own business strategy, and its own presence in the market, each seller has his or her own set of challenges and problems. For this reason, every sales position requires its own particular combination of characteristics for the salesperson to become a top seller in that field at that time. Although it's unlikely that any one salesperson possesses all of the traits discussed in this chapter, high producers generally exhibit a majority of these tendencies that set them apart from the average seller.

How can you emulate and assimilate the characteristics of the most successful salespeople?

SET SPECIFIC SHORT-TERM AND LONG-TERM GOALS

Set high personal and business goals and make a commitment to achieve them. Make each goal specific and give it a top priority in your life. Monitor your progress regularly. If your short-term goal is to sell $100,000 worth of computers this month, and at the end of the second week you only have $25,000 in orders and few if any outstanding prospects, you probably will not meet your goal. Don't wait until the last minute to accelerate your efforts! Work harder and smarter by using synergistic sales techniques that bring people together for the good of each participating party. Change your sales approach, network, and increase your direct-mail effort and/or your telemarketing campaign. Do not expect an order to miraculously appear, enabling you to meet your goal. (If fate is kind and an order should unexpectedly come in, it will make next month's goal all the easier to achieve.)

TAKE THE INITIATIVE

Being self-motivated is sometimes easier said than done, but it helps to have a strong ego and like what you're doing.

When a football team plays an important game, all team members are typically enthusiastic. Each knows that he can count on his teammates to play at peak performance for the benefit of the team. Each knows how dependent he is on his teammates. No one player can throw the ball, catch the ball, block, tackle, and make touchdowns. In sales, though, you can create your own destiny. You can play all of the positions yourself and make each and every touchdown single-handedly.

Imagine that the football is your product. As the quarterback, you pass the ball to your prospect. All eyes are on you as you deliver your sales presentation. Just as an offensive lineman blocks for the quarterback, you knock your competitors out of consideration. Successfully closing the sale is just like outwitting your opponents and running into the end zone for a touchdown. A professional football player is motivated by his love of the sport, the challenge to win each and every game, earning the big salary, and gaining the respect of the other players, his coach, and the fans. He plays with a sense of conviction. The most successful salespeople are motivated by the same types of things. *In sales, winning is everything.* Setting goals will help you acquire and maintain the self-motivation necessary for your success.

STRIVE FOR ACHIEVEMENT

The achievement-oriented salesperson works with a winning attitude, a positive outlook, and a sense of commitment. Many salespeople bring bad habits to the job. They start late, quit early, and find a million reasons to postpone a sales call. They go through their paces with a general malaise and no sense of urgency. Each of us will experience an occasional bad day, but a salesperson who is not achievement-oriented can make every day a bad day.

Concentrate on achieving your goals. Put on your tunnel visors if that's what it takes, and leave your personal problems and negative baggage behind you. Make your selling time work for you.

DISCIPLINE YOURSELF

If you want to win consistently, you must be self-disciplined. This requires a little effort and a lot of determination.

Most of us perform well under a structured system. A young girl attending summer camp drags herself out of bed each morning at the insistence of her camp director. She cleans her plate off and puts her breakfast dishes in the assigned staging area. She arrives at each planned activity on time. She participates in arts and crafts as do the rest of the girls. She even writes home to Mom and Dad every week. Of course, Mom and Dad may not realize that every Friday morning at 11:00 A.M. the counselors hand out paper, pens, envelopes, and stamps and instruct the campers to write home. Letter writing is pretty easy under these circumstances.

A salesperson working outside of the office is not awakened by a blast of reveille from the sales manager each morning. Few salespeople have their daily sales calls and other activities preprogrammed for them by someone else. Self-discipline requires properly planning your day and using time to your best advantage. If you have a few minutes before an appointment, don't make small talk with the receptionist or work the crossword puzzle in the newspaper. Compose a thank-you note, work on a strategy for a new account, make a few telephone calls, or complete your call reports.

Suffer the pain of self-discipline instead of the pain of regret. If you fail to schedule your itinerary properly or disregard it and approach your work without a sense of dedication and purpose, you probably will not have a successful sales career. At the very least, you will disappoint yourself because you'll probably fail to meet your goals. More than likely, you'll also disappoint (and probably anger) your sales manager for his or her expectations won't be met. If you want to win consistently, you must be self-disciplined.

DEMONSTRATE PERSISTENCE

Many of the most successful salespeople attribute their success to their unceasing persistence. Ray Kroc, whose success with McDonald's is legendary, kept the following maxim, attributed to Calvin Coolidge, prominently displayed in his office:

Nothing in the world can take the place of persistence. Talent will not; nothing is more common than unsuccessful men with talent. Genius will not; unrewarded genius is almost a proverb. Education will not; the world is full of educated derelicts. Persistence and determination alone are omnipotent.

Few characteristics are as important to the success of a superseller as persistence. If you really believe in what you are selling, a "no" answer is simply unacceptable. The most difficult tasks can be accomplished if you are persistent. One of my favorite sales anecdotes illustrates this best:

> "You should feel proud of yourself, young fellow," the executive disclosed to the life insurance agent. "I've refused to see seven insurance salespeople today."
> "I know," replied the agent. "I'm them."

I cannot tell you how many times I was prepared to throw in the towel only to then have the prospect give me the order. *Persistence can be your key to superstardom,* so don't give up.

BE ASSERTIVE

If you have a driving, task-oriented personality, being assertive may be easy for you. On the other hand, if you are basically analytical or amiable, you may find it difficult to be assertive. I know one very successful salesman who is basically shy and introverted, yet his enthusiasm for the service he offers makes him shine and radiate confidence in a sales presentation, thus making him more assertive. In other words, a strong belief in your product may help you overcome self-doubt or lack of confidence.

An assertive individual usually is confident and positive by nature. Unlike aggressiveness, which may be based in anger or hostility and result in a win/lose type of situation to a prospect or customer, assertiveness enables both sides to win. If you lack this important characteristic, there are scores of assertiveness-training seminars and books that will teach you how to project your self-confidence.

An assertive presentation provides the salesperson with a sense of authority and importance. If you present yourself in a self-confident manner, there is nonverbal affirmation of the superiority of your product or service and company and an acceptance by your prospect that you must know what you're talking about. Customers want you to care about their needs and solve their problems. In fact, they want you to care enough to overcome their objections and their lack of understanding. Assertiveness works toward that end for it is difficult to buy a service from someone who is apathetic.

The more you know about your product or service, company, marketplace, and customer, the greater your level of confidence will be. The more confident you are, the greater your level of assertion and the more persuasive your sales presentation will be. As a result, you'll sell more. The successful salesperson identifies a problem, and then with a great deal of confidence and authority, she offers a workable solution. The outcome is almost always the same: positive customer action, more orders for your product, and great success for the seller.

BE DECISIVE

Many people suffer from indecisiveness because they're afraid of failure. Rather than risk the effects of a bad decision, they do nothing at all. Demonstrate your resolve, and you could help an indecisive prospect make the decision to buy your service. Money-back guarantees work because the salesperson is basically carrying the weight of the decision for the customer. The consumer says to himself, "If I am wrong, my decision won't hurt me because I can virtually undo any damage I may experience as a result."

If you speak with authority and appear to be decisive, you will minimize the anxiety that your prospect may otherwise feel. If you appear to be indecisive, his anxiety will rise, and you will make him question the wisdom of purchasing from you.

SHOW EMPATHY

If you really identify with your prospect and understand his situation, feelings, and motives, you will significantly improve your chances of closing your sale.

As a salesperson, you must get inside each customer's head to see you and your products from his point of view. Only then can you know what it will take for him to make the decision to buy. If you understand his needs and concerns, you probably will be able to motivate him to action and help satisfy his needs, and he will help you satisfy yours.

Be sensitive to your customer's situation. If a prospect is struggling to make ends meet, money is a very big issue with her. Put her mind at ease. Don't increase her anxiety level by trying to sell her your most expensive deluxe model. Sell her the starter unit instead, and let her give you ten leads who can possibly afford your deluxe model. Be sensitive to her feelings. It is easy for you to apply the pressure and make the big sale today, but she's the one who will have to make the payments for the next three years.

The most successful sellers use empathy hand in hand with consultative selling techniques. Ask a prospect what his or her goals are and then show how your product or service can help achieve those goals. Find out what your prospect's problems are and then work toward a solution.

Avoid the temptation to tell customers only what you want them to hear, or what you think they want to hear.

STAY MENTALLY FLEXIBLE

If one sales approach does not work, try another. Keep trying until you discover the most effective approach. You must be able to think on your feet and improvise. If you find a new fact or uncover a different way to present a concept, incorporate it into your sales presentations and closing techniques. Develop the ability to accommodate changing conditions and changes of mind.

Many external factors will require mental flexibility on your part. Many a long-standing customer has been lost to the competition because a particular buyer moved, was promoted, or retired, and the salesperson couldn't adapt to the new situation or didn't make the changes the new buyer demanded. If yesterday's relationships and ways of doing business no longer work, abandon them. Each day is a new day and may require a fresh approach. Enjoy the challenges of each new day and find ways to reorganize your perceptions to meet the demands placed on you. If you are too set in your ways and refuse to change with the tide, you undoubtedly will drown in the sea of inflexibility.

USE YOUR CREATIVITY

Creative thinking is characterized by originality and expressiveness. Imagination is essential to meet the challenges each prospect presents. Finding solutions to problems requires a salesperson to think creatively to come up with the answers that have eluded your prospect and perhaps your competition.

If you lack imagination and expressiveness, tap the creative resources. Read books by Lee Iacocca, Harvey

Mackay, Og Mandino, Tom Hopkins, Zig Ziglar, Anthony Robbins, and other motivational writers and speakers. If you do not have a particular attribute yourself, do not despair. By investing a little time studying the masters, you can attain your sales and career goals by simply taking advantage of their years of experience!

BE TRUTHFUL AND PRINCIPLE BASED

In *The 7 Habits of Highly Effective People* (New York: Fireside/Simon & Schuster), author Stephen R. Covey talks about truthfulness and his observations that most successful people are principle based. As a principle-centered person, you look at all your options and take all factors into consideration before arriving at the best solution. Being principle centered and truthful will help you create a steady life foundation without all the extreme emotional peaks and valleys typically experienced by people who have not centered their lives around sound principles.

For example, if you are money based, your life revolves around money. When an investment goes bad, your year is ruined. Your emotional well-being is tied to your bank account. When your account is low, you are low; when your account is high, you are high. The end result is that you become emotionally bankrupt. Covey discusses the importance of centering our lives on correct principles, which are deeply rooted in each of us and, in most cases, originate with good parenting. These principles are reinforced as we develop our character early in childhood and throughout our life.

We develop an appreciation and acceptance for fundamental truths. For example, we know that lying is wrong, stealing is bad, and hurting other people is unacceptable behavior. If you choose your actions based on your knowledge of correct principles, you will build both your personal and business relationships on a solid foundation upon which the highest goals may be achieved.

DEVELOP A GOOD SENSE OF HUMOR

Most successful salespeople have a sense of humor. Remember that the journey can be as important, rewarding, and pleasant as reaching your destination, so don't take yourself so seriously that you don't have any fun! Most people like doing business with people who are fun to be around and enjoy life.

BE ACCOUNTABLE

The superstars accept responsibility for their actions. Be responsive to any problems a customer may have and make sure that you follow up after closing a sale.

USE NEURO-LINGUISTIC PROGRAMMING

The top sellers have developed the ability to match their styles with the styles of their prospects. They use pacing to make each prospect feel at ease.

To learn the basics in mirroring the styles and mannerisms of your prospects, see Chapter 5, "Win with Neuro-Linguistic Programming," and practice the techniques until they become second nature to you.

KNOW YOUR PRODUCT OR SERVICE INSIDE OUT

Know your product completely. As a highly knowledgeable professional, your customers will rely on you as a valuable consultant and seek your advice on solving their business problems.

MAINTAIN A THIRST FOR KNOWLEDGE

Read sales and marketing books, industry newsletters, and trade papers. Attend seminars, workshops, and trade shows on a regular basis. Look for opportunities to acquire new skills. Stay current with the latest developments in your field as well as with the latest local, state, national, and international news.

LEARN TO COMMUNICATE WELL
ON MANY LEVELS

Supersalespeople excel in the area of communication. In their book *Smart Moves* (Reading, Mass.: Addison-Wesley Publishing Company, Inc.), Sam Deep and Lyle Sussman suggest the following ways to learn about your own communication style:

1. Ask for specific feedback from those close to you.
2. Carefully observe the verbal and nonverbal reactions of others to you.
3. Record yourself on both videotape and audiotape and study each.
4. Check out your body image in a mirror.
5. Listen to yourself as you speak and hear how you sound to others.

Remember that communication is a two-way flow of information that involves both giving and receiving. According to Deep and Sussman, your tone of voice and body language communicate more than 90 percent of your message, so try to be aware of the nonverbal messages you are sending and stay attuned to the nonverbal cues of others. (For more on communication skills, see Chapter 9, "Power Presentations That Work.")

During my more than twenty-year sales career, I have sold more than $1 billion worth of products and services. My sales career has produced millions of dollars in earnings. If I were to tell you the reasons for that success, I would place four key items at the top of my list: *enthusiasm, synergistic sales, hard work,* and *packaging the sales opportunity.*

SHOW ENTHUSIASM

Ralph Waldo Emerson wrote, "Nothing great was ever achieved without enthusiasm." If you had a vaccine that prevented people from contracting AIDS, would you be pretty enthusiastic about selling such a product? I think most salespeople would be extremely excited about saving lives and being part of a program that helps eliminate one of the most dreaded diseases of this century.

Your product may not have so dramatic a demand, but stop and think about what the sales of your product really mean. No matter what product or service you sell, it affects the lives of others.

Let's assume that you are selling a simple kitchen appliance. For illustration purposes, any product or service could be used, but let's assume that you sell Bunn coffee makers. As a youngster, you probably did not dream about working for Bunn-O-Matic when you grew up, but you're selling a product that is well accepted in the marketplace and is being distributed by approximately thirty distributors in about 100 countries. Thanks to a good advertising program, most retail stores feel a compelling need to put your product on the shelf. For the purpose of this illustration, suppose that your only real competitor is Mr. Coffee and that all of the other competitors put together probably add up to less than 6 percent of the marketplace.

Stop and realize what your mission is: to sell more coffee makers than anyone else in the world. Your challenge would be to develop a sales campaign that would give you the total market. You could get really enthusiastic about cutting into your competitor's business. The psychological rewards would be phenomenal. Perhaps you could discount the coffee maker and increase the disposable-filter charge as a marketing strategy. Perhaps you might negotiate a deal with gourmet coffee-bean importers and mail-order houses to credit their customers with a $1 coupon credit toward the purchase of a Bunn coffee maker with the purchase of each pound of coffee beans. Maybe you could make a similar arrangement with major grocery stores.

You must realize that the sale of coffee makers increases your company's profits, which yields dividends for investors in your company. Each of your sales produces jobs.

What you are doing is important, and you should be enthusiastic about your job and the beneficial effect you have on your customers, your company and its stockholders, your community, and your country. Don't forget: Until the sale is made, nothing happens. That's something to get enthusiastic about.

PRACTICE SYNERGISTIC SELLING

The American Heritage Dictionary defines synergism as "the action of two or more substances, organs, or organisms to achieve an effect of which each is individually incapable; working together." When I was selling electrical wind generators to investors, I found that only one prospect out of thirty-seven I contacted each week had sufficient tax liability and/or financial resources to acquire a wind turbine that sold for $150,000. Of course, I only made presentations to prospects who had been prescreened, so I knew that each prospect was earning more than $100,000 per year. My average sales production was one wind turbine per week, resulting in a $15,000 commission for an annual income of $780,000. Not a bad living actually.

After walking away from thirty-six potential investors each week who simply did not qualify to own a wind turbine, I decided to try a synergistic sales technique that created a $2-million pay raise for me that year.

I held a small seminar for financial planners and certified public accountants (CPAs) at a Los Angeles hotel. My two-hour seminar was designed to show financial planners and others entrusted with other people's money how to acquire an asset with tax dollars. I knew that each attendee could form a small investment group comprised of his or her wealthier clients who had appreciable tax liability. The investment group could form a limited or general partnership and *collectively* buy a wind turbine.

I discounted the wind turbine 20 percent to the financial planners and CPAs, making their price $120,000, and they would sell them to their clients for $150,000. The group then would split the cost proportionately among its members and split the gains as well. If this concept worked, I also could invite the thirty-six prospects I was talking to each week to join one of these investment groups. Thus, I could convert every prospect into a bona fide customer regardless of his or her personal tax liability or financial status.

During the seminar, I explained to the attendees that a basic wind turbine stood ten stories high (100 feet), weighed more than 30,000 pounds, and was computer controlled. If the wind was blowing out of the southwest at 270 degrees, the computer would tell the blades which direction to point and angle the nacelle (the unit to which blades are mounted) to give the blades maximum wind exposure, thus optimizing the energy output.

Each wind turbine generated more than 400,000 kilo-watt-hours (kwh) of energy per year. The Public Utilities Regulatory Policy Act of 1978 required the utilities to purchase all alternative energy generated *at their highest avoided cost.* Avoided cost is that amount of money the utility saves by not burning fossil fuels (gas and oil) and by purchasing energy produced by wind and water (hy-droelectricity). For instance, if gas cost the utility four cents per kwh, and oil cost ten cents per kwh, the utility company was required to pay ten cents for the alternative energy produced.

If the wind turbine owner multiplied 400,000 by ten cents, his or her return on investment (ROI) would be $40,000 per year. Not a bad return on a $150,000 invest-ment. "Try to find a financial institution that would pay your clients a 26.6 percent annualized interest rate," I would tell the seminar attendees. If a financial institution would give that rate of return, the client most probably would have to leave his or her entire $150,000 in an ac-count for a specified period of time.

If an investment group were to be formed, however, the clients did *not* have to put up the $150,000; they would earn the same interest as if they had; and, they'd own a wind turbine with tax dollars. At the same time, the fed-eral government gave investors a 15 percent energy tax credit and a 10 percent investment tax credit. Many states were giving investors an additional 25 percent energy tax credit. After the taxpayer took all of the normal deductions and arrived at a fair income tax, he or she could withhold that payment and use it for an alternative-energy invest-ment. This incentive program designed by the federal and state governments to encourage investments in alternative energy meant that for many investors 50 percent of the investment came from tax dollars.

To sweeten the investment even more, the federal government allowed the investor to write off the investment in five years with an accelerated depreciation cost-recovery system, giving the investment club the ability to write off $30,000 per year in depreciation. If the investment club put down 50 percent of the $150,000 ($75,000), each member could amend his or her own individual tax return and either go back three years for a refund on taxes already paid or withhold his or her tax payment that year and invest it in a wind turbine instead. While investors were making payments on the remaining $75,000 balance, they would be enjoying the depreciation deduction. The investment clubs were legally using *tax dollars* to acquire $150,000 in assets.

All of a sudden, my sales closings went from one in thirty-seven to *fifteen out of thirty-seven*, and my annual earnings went from nearly $800,000 a year to *almost $3 million a year*. The only thing I did differently was recruit partners who could form and manage groups of customers. Everybody wanted to take advantage of this wonderful tax-shelter opportunity, but only a few had the tax liability or financial resources to buy. I used *synergistic sales* to provide my customers with the opportunities previously reserved for only the very rich.

One of the most successful salespeople in this country resides in San Francisco. He inherited a small printing company in Miami from his uncle, a great printer but a poor businessman. When Jim arrived in Miami, he was confronted with nervous customers who had made cash deposits for deliveries that were late. He assisted the three remaining employees to make good on the jobs that needed to be delivered. The creditors were less than amiable, and many were insisting on immediate payment or they were going to place the business in involuntary bankruptcy. After obtaining a small loan, Jim was able to satisfy the creditors.

Jim then realized that he had inherited a nice little business. The company's building had a ten-year lease at favorable rates, and the printing equipment was state of the art. The business lacked only one thing: *sales.*

Jim decided to create a proprietary product. He envisioned an office-building guide for people who wanted to rent office space in the greater Miami area. A 100-page, four-color directory of the top fifty office buildings, the guide would include a full-page photograph of a building on one page and a corresponding full-page advertisement on the opposite page. Each time an office-building owner or manager purchased a four-color page for $4,000, he or she would get the facing page free. The directory would be distributed to every commercial real estate office in town, the chamber of commerce, and corporate-facilities managers. For less than $335 per month—less than the price of a similar yellow-pages advertisement—the building owner would have a two-page, four-color advertisement distributed directly to his or her target market: the people who rent office space.

Within one month, Jim had cash deposits from more than fifty building owners and managers. Jim printed 5,000 copies of the directory at a cost to him of $5 per copy, including layout, color separations, and typesetting. He spent $25,000 and collected $200,000. His directory had become a successful reality.

Jim used synergistic selling to bring people together for the common good. He gave the Realtors, facility managers, and chamber of commerce what they needed: an easy reference guide that included vital information such as cost per square foot, location, special services, and security coverage. The building owners and managers got what they needed: effective advertising targeted to their markets at a reasonable price. Jim gave the prospect looking for office space a concise, informative, beautiful guide to the office buildings in the greater Miami area.

Top sellers want what is best for their customers. Because synergistic selling brings people together for the common good, it *works*.

Another extraordinary sales professional used synergistic sales to amass her fortune in Detroit. As an independent representative, Susan was selling business forms for three companies. She earned a 10 percent commission on two of her lines of computer forms and 15 percent on the third. Earning a low six-figure income, she lived in a modest suburban home just outside of Detroit with her aging parents. Having sold business forms for more than ten years, she knew her client base and competition extremely well. A great networker, she enjoyed attending industry conventions and association meetings in her midwestern region.

At a Grand Rapids association meeting, Susan overheard a conversation about the rising cost of paper products. One participant wondered aloud, "Why don't customers in the area form a cooperative so that they can enjoy lower prices by buying in greater quantities?" The seed was planted and Susan went to work. She called all of her customers to ask if they would be interested in saving 5 to 10 percent on all of their business-form purchases. Of course, each responded affirmatively. Susan arbitrarily formed four separate buying groups to pool their purchases of generic forms that did not require personalization. She then began making calls to companies where she had previously been unable to compete head-on and invited them to join her co-op. Many prospects who had been using the competitors' forms readily switched to buying through the group because the group's prices were cheaper than the competitors' prices and Susan had a good reputation in the industry.

Susan had enjoyed a 17 percent market share, respectable by most marketing standards depending on whether or not you have a proprietary product. With her co-op venture, her market share soared to 64 percent! Her income went from $180,000 per year to more than $1 million per year. Susan learned what synergistic selling is all about.

PACKAGE YOUR SALES OPPORTUNITY ATTRACTIVELY

A supersalesperson in Atlanta earns $150,000 per month. He is one of many multilevel marketing professionals who has learned how to use synergistic selling.

Using a large pad of paper clipped to an easel, George opens his seminars by asking, "Who can help me form the perfect company? It must operate legally, it must earn huge profits, and it must not require too much work." Once his audience understands the ground rules, he opens up the floor for audience input.

One person yells out, "It should have no employees. Employees are a pain in the neck and cause ulcers." Someone else cries out, "I want a company that does not require inventory. Inventories take space and cost money." A gentleman in the back of the room stands up and says, "I do not want to go to an office every day. I want to work out of my home." Someone else says that she does not want to worry about people not paying their bills.

The feedback continues until George has about thirty items listed to help him form this imaginary new company. His audience has participated in establishing a company in which they want to take part. What company do you suppose meets the criteria the audience has established? It should come as no surprise that it's a distributorship with George's multilevel marketing firm.

George tells his seminar attendees that if they simply pay the new distributor fee and fill out the appropriate applications, they could enjoy the following advantages of owning their own distributorship:

- Working out of your own home
- No employees
- No inventory
- Administrative work handled by the company
- Accounting work performed by the company
- All sales materials provided by the company
- No manufacturing problems
- Earnings from the work of others
- Great retirement income
- No management problems
- All-cash sales
- No collection or bad-debt problems
- Tax deductions on home and auto
- Distributorship can be sold as an asset

Interestingly enough, every single desire of the audience was met by becoming a distributor for George's company. As a result of his seminars, George has signed tens of thousands of new distributors. In two years, he has joined the growing ranks of millionaires in the United States.

One of the key characteristics shared by these super-achievers is the ability to package their product, service, or company in a unique and highly desirable way. Ask anyone if he or she wants to own an electricity-generating wind turbine and see how few people run for their wallets. You can guess what the response is when you ask the same person if he or she wants to acquire a $150,000 asset that will produce an income for many years to come at no cost.

Why did Jim's office directory bring in millions of dollars? He produced a proprietary product, but he used *sales packaging* to sell it. His competitor offered standard printing services such as brochures, stationery, and business cards. Jim offered perhaps a once-in-a-lifetime opportunity to be listed as one of the top fifty office buildings in

Miami. He gave each building owner the chance to have his or her advertisement distributed to people who make renting decisions or refer potential tenants, all for less than the cost of a comparable yellow-pages display advertisement. The better the sales packaging, the higher the close rate.

Packaging your sales opportunity correctly is all-important. The experts smartly position their products and services so that *everyone wins.* As I did when selling wind turbines, all Susan did with her business-forms co-op was to help her customers save money by bringing them together for the common good. She sold business forms at the lowest price in town without having to compromise quality or service.

Yes, each of these dynamic sales professionals displays similar characteristics. All of them are drivers. They are assertive, determined, and hardworking, but they also work *smart.*

At the age of twenty-four, I was selling printed circuit boards. The owners of the company had arranged for a modest industrial development loan from the Business Development Association of Eveleth, Minnesota. The association had been formed by a group of local businesspeople who wanted to attract industry to their economically devastated city. At one time, the city enjoyed great affluence while iron-ore mines contributed to the steel production supporting the World War II effort. As iron-ore removal progressed at a rapid rate, one mine after another was forced to shut down until there were no operative mines left. Miners, their families, and all of the support service people began to move out of the area. Retail stores began to close, and the future growth prospects for Eveleth were bleak. Out of desperation, the business-development association was formed, and precious dollars were offered to anyone who could bring jobs to Eveleth.

The loan would enable us to purchase equipment to manufacture printed circuit boards. The city gave us free use of a high school building that had not been in operation for twenty years because of the declining student enrollment, and we were given free employee training by the state vocational-training department. Start-up money, use of a building for free, and training—wow, what a deal! My partners could purchase the silk-screening presses, raw materials, acid tanks, electroplating equipment, drill presses, and all the specialized equipment necessary to manufacture printed circuit boards. My job was to sell the finished product to manufacturers that used printed circuit boards in their products (television sets, organs, telephones, radios, CB radios, and a host of other electronic products).

After I moved my family and myself to Eveleth, the anticipated funding did not materialize. Investors in the association changed their minds, and only half of the promised funds were released. My partners were ready to close the doors on our new enterprise. This dark moment became my first opportunity to use a sales-packaging concept to create a successful business.

I contacted the more than 100 companies whose equipment and supplies we needed to open our doors. I proposed that *our company sell their equipment for them.* Not buy—sell. I proposed to accept the best model from each company and install it in my showcase facility. I agreed to invite prospective printed circuit manufacturers to visit this totally operational manufacturing facility and demonstrate my suppliers' best equipment in an actual user setting. I also would provide technical training to those who purchased their equipment from me. With very few exceptions, everyone embraced the idea, and we got our equipment for free. Herein lies part of the secret that I nearly took to my grave in March of 1985. More on that later.

While Motorola was setting up its own in-house manufacturing facility, I sold them my printed circuit boards. Not only was Motorola buying my product, but it was buying the very equipment I used to manufacture my product! It seemed that sales were coming from every corner of the earth. We actually made more money selling equipment than we made selling printed circuit boards. Of course, all of the revenue was appreciated, whatever the source.

We soon became nationally recognized experts in printed circuit production. Each week, hundreds of corporate visitors filled Eveleth's motel rooms, restaurants, and bars. Retail merchants were experiencing major increases in their sales. The taxes paid by our employees helped the city to improve services to the citizenry. Suddenly, the association's investors who had reneged on their original investment commitments changed their minds and wanted to invest in our business, but, of course, it was too late. The ones who had invested earned three times their money in less than a year.

Packaging your sale correctly is critical. What could have been a tragedy for me became a real blessing. If all the association's investors had met their contribution obligations, my showcase manufacturing concept never would have been born. Consider all your options when packaging your sales concept, and look at each problem as simply a new opportunity ready to be exploited. Package it properly, and wonderful things will begin to happen.

Lee Iacocca once sold automobiles for Ford Motor Company in its fleet sales department. Years later, his career path took him to the chief executive officer's chair at Chrysler Corporation. In 1979, Chrysler forecast that its losses would climb to more than $1 billion. The banks refused to extend any more credit to Chrysler. The corporation was frequently within hours of bankruptcy. The business climate at Chrysler was desperate, and the future of one of America's major corporations was in the balance.

It appeared that Chrysler's continued existence would depend largely on the goodwill of its suppliers, the United Auto Workers union, and the federal government. Iacocca and the management of Chrysler smartly positioned their sales opportunity by convincing Congress that plant closings would have an extraordinary impact on the U.S. economy. While it was hard to feel compassion for a monolith like Chrysler, the 4,500 Chrysler dealers, the 19,000 suppliers with $800 million in accounts receivable from Chrysler, and the huge number of union members who would be out of jobs were *real people* who would suffer tremendously if Chrysler went under.

Experts estimated that a Chrysler bankruptcy would mean a decline in the gross national product of 0.5 percent, an increase in the U.S. unemployment rate of 0.5 to 1.09 percent, and a negative impact of approximately $1.5 billion on the U.S. trade balance. The potential annual tax loss to the country was estimated at $500 million, and the government could have been responsible for $1.5 billion in welfare checks.

It is people and their ideas who succeed or fail, *not* companies. Instead of declaring bankruptcy, Iacocca was able to distribute large economic losses to Chrysler's constituency and to win concessions from all of them. The union pared $462.5 million from its contract and accepted a pay freeze that cost an additional $522 million in wages. In turn, Chrysler gave in to certain nonwage demands made by the union. Chrysler's suppliers accepted delayed payments and $36 million in price breaks. The U.S. banks and financial institutions were asked to give concessions of $500 million ($400 million in new loans and $100 million in old debt), and the foreign banks were to provide $150 million in new loans and credit. The banks later would be asked for $600 million through a conversion of debt to preferred stock. Chrysler's total obligation to the federal government was $1.2 billion. Iacocca urged us all to work together to "Buy American," and we bought his dream.

Every successful sales professional has been told at one time or another how lucky he is or how she just happened to be in the right place at the right time. The business success of the superstars of the sales world is the result of much more than luck or timing. Each possesses many of the same basic attributes as their peers: initiative, drive, optimism, enthusiasm, persistence, decisiveness, empathy, goal orientedness, self-discipline, creativity, achievement orientedness, a thirst for knowledge, and a great belief in himself or herself. Each thinks well on his or her feet. Each is accountable for his or her actions, and integrity is an important part of each sales professional's principle-centered lives. Each has developed the ability to mirror his or her customers and knows his or her product completely. Each understands the benefits of synergistic sales and the importance of wisely conceptualizing and then positioning the product or service.

WORK HARD

Do you recognize yourself in this elite group? If not, take heart. Most of these traits can be learned, enhanced, or acquired through *hard work*. As Vidal Sassoon learned from one of his teachers, "The only place that success comes before work is in the dictionary."

WORK ASSIGNMENT

Study five successful salespeople whom you know and make a list of their characteristics. See how many attributes you can identify. The sixth person I want you to honestly analyze by listing characteristics is *yourself*. By doing so, you will gain some personal insight into your strengths and weaknesses. When you determine what characteristics you need to become more successful, you can work to develop them or learn to compensate for them in other ways.

4
What Makes You and Your Customers Tick?

"Sometimes a cigar is just a cigar."

—Sigmund Freud

The American Heritage Dictionary defines personality as "the totality of qualities and traits, as of character or behavior, that are peculiar to an individual person . . . the pattern of collective character, behavioral, temperamental, emotional, and mental traits of an individual." Personality specialists assume that variations in an individual's behavior are the result of individual personal traits. The behavior is based on interactions of a wide variety of factors that the personality-assessment specialist tries to measure objectively.

WHY IS THERE SO MUCH INTEREST IN PERSONALITIES?

Why is personality assessment of such great concern to philosophers, psychologists, businesspeople, the clergy, and sales professionals? Is it to understand man's behavior better or to predict his behavior and try to control him? Philosophers, psychologists, and clergy probably are more interested with the former, while the businessperson and sales professional are more concerned with the latter.

Personality assessment is not new. The ancient Greeks believed that one's health depended on the right balance of bodily fluids. The phlegmatic personality was stable and introverted. These individuals were passive, cautious, thoughtful, calm, sullen, reserved, and pessimistic. The melancholic personality was unstable and introverted, with some traits of moodiness and high levels of anxiety. The sanguine personality was stable, carefree, and extroverted, exhibiting leadership qualities and an easygoing nature. The choleric temperament was described as unstable and changeable but extroverted, optimistic, and active. Another more modern morphological theory belonged to Ernst Kretschmer, who espoused that personalities were based on being one of three body types: pyknic (short and stocky), asthenic/leptosomic (slender), or athletic.

With the advent of Freudian psychoanalysis and Sigmund Freud's belief that childhood experiences and sexual motivation affect the personality, emphasis shifted from the physiological to the psychogenic (originating in the mind). Carl Jung, an analytical psychologist and associate of Freud's, believed that the mind has four basic functions: thinking, feeling, sensation, and intuition; one or more of these functions predominates in each individual, making up his or her personality. Prominent psychologist Alfred Adler pioneered the "individual" approach to personality, citing every individual's uniqueness and personal struggle toward self-realization. Many other theories of personality were postulated during the first half of the twentieth century.

More recent theories are more eclectic, with theorists

picking and choosing from the wealth of information that has accumulated over the years rather than setting forth one all-encompassing master theory. Two major emphases continue:

1. Each individual shares common characteristics or traits with others.
2. Each individual is unique because of the specific combination and degree of manifestation of these traits.

The theories of personality are based on an attempt to be nothing less than scientific. Frequently, however, there are weaknesses in how personality traits are measured, often because the trait or traits to be measured are inadequately defined. If at all possible, personality traits are best measured by *direct observation*.

The interview is one of the most frequently used methods to evaluate personality. It provides an opportunity to gather information on life history and current status, yet allows the interviewer to directly observe an individual's behavior. Behavioral observation is another evaluation tool, and the subject may or may not be aware that he or she is being observed.

Personality inventories usually are easy to administer and easy to score, and they are objective. But they are frequently restrictive in scope. The Minnesota Multiphasic Personality Inventory (MMPI), the California Psychological Inventory (CPI), the Eysenck Personality Inventory, and the Edwards Personality Preference Schedule are all examples of valid self-reporting inventories.

Projective techniques also may be used to measure personality traits. These may take the form of associative methods (reacting to inkblots or to specific words), construction techniques (drawing a person), completion methods (finishing a sentence), or ordering or choice methods (arranging a set of pictures).

So what is the value of understanding your own personality and the personalities of others? If you can determine a prospect's personality, you can present your products and services in the most acceptable way. If through personality analysis a prospect's behavior can be predicted, you can arrange your sales presentations and closing techniques to allow for a predictable result—the sale. For example, you would be ill-advised to present a nontechnical product in an analytical format to a task-oriented Assertive personality. Conversely, if you attempt to sell only benefits to an Analytical buyer, your chance of success will be greatly reduced. This will become more apparent to you as you read further.

To make the most of your selling opportunities, you must understand your personality as well. If you are a Friendly type of person, you may be inclined to engage in a great deal of friendly conversation, and you probably will make sales to the few amiable people who, like you, judge themselves by the number of friends they have rather than by other yardsticks. Each personality has its corresponding strengths and weaknesses. A salesman with an Assertive personality may sell a high percentage of his prospects because he expresses enthusiasm, a power of conviction, and product knowledge, and he seldom hesitates to ask for the order. But he also can lose a lot of sales if he becomes too pushy, arrogant, abrupt, and to the point. He may make sloppy presentations and may not take the time to accurately determine his prospect's precise needs.

Because so many descriptive terms could relate to personality, the potential variety of types of theories is astronomical. Everyone seems to have a favorite theory, and I'm no different. So that you can better understand yourself, I have designed a personality-assessment checklist with which you will be able to determine your personality. Respond *honestly*. No one needs to see this assessment but you, so don't try to answer as you think you *should*. Scoring involves analyzing pairs of opposing dimensions of personality, such as dominance and submission, introversion and extroversion.

After you have completed this checklist and have ascertained which personality type you are, I will discuss the attributes along with the strengths and weaknesses associated with each of the basic personalities. I also will teach you how to quickly assess the personalities of others. Once you learn these personality-assessment techniques, you will be able to persuasively present your product or service in a way most acceptable to each personality type.

The basic techniques discussed here are based on years of field research, but the perfection of these techniques is an art. After a few months of practice, you should be able to assess a prospect's basic personality within a few short minutes after meeting him or her. Moreover, you should be able to make that determination over the telephone. By determining your prospect's personality before your appointment date, you will be able to prepare suitable sales materials in advance and substantially increase your chances of closing the sale.

PERSONALITY ASSESSMENT CHECKLIST

Please check off the words that best describe you. Then add up the number of check marks *in each column* and write the total at the bottom of each column.

1	2	3	4
☐ INDIFFERENT	☐ COMPETITIVE	☐ UNDISCIPLINED	☐ SOFT-SPOKEN
☐ ALOOF	☐ CONSPICUOUS	ABOUT TIME	☐ SLOW PACE
☐ UNCOMMUNICATIVE	☐ GAMBLER	☐ IMPULSIVE	☐ FLAT VOICE
☐ GUARDED	☐ AGGRESSIVE	☐ OPEN	☐ INDIFFERENT
☐ CAREFUL	☐ OPINIONATED	☐ WARM	HANDSHAKE
☐ DISCIPLINED	☐ TAKE-CHARGE	☐ AMIABLE	☐ UNCLEAR ABOUT
ABOUT TIME	ATTITUDE	☐ COMMUNICATIVE	WHAT IS NEEDED
☐ USES FACTS	☐ BRAZEN	☐ USES OPINIONS	☐ ASKS QUESTIONS
☐ FORMAL DRESS	☐ TENDS TO USE	☐ INFORMAL DRESS	☐ LETS OTHERS TAKE
AND SPEECH	POWER	AND SPEECH	SOCIAL INITIATIVE
☐ MEASURED	☐ TAKES SOCIAL	☐ DRAMATIC	☐ TENDS TO AVOID
OPINIONS AND	INITIATIVE	OPINIONS AND	USE OF POWER
ACTIONS	☐ MAKES	ACTIONS	☐ SUPPORTIVE
☐ STRICT	STATEMENTS	☐ PERMISSIVE	☐ COOPERATIVE
☐ DISCIPLINED	☐ LOUD VOICE	☐ FLEXIBLE	☐ DELIBERATE
☐ RATIONAL	☐ QUICK PACE	ATTITUDES	ACTIONS
DECISION MAKING	☐ EXPRESSIVE VOICE	☐ EMOTIONAL	☐ RISK AVOIDER
☐ SEEMS DIFFICULT	☐ FIRM HANDSHAKE	DECISION MAKING	☐ QUIET
TO GET TO KNOW	☐ CLEAR IDEA OF	☐ SEEMS EASY TO	☐ MODERATE
☐ DEMANDING OF	NEED	GET TO KNOW	OPINIONS
SELF AND OTHERS		☐ EASYGOING WITH	☐ INDECISIVE
☐ CLINICAL AND		SELF AND OTHERS	
BUSINESSLIKE		☐ PERSONAL AND	
		FRIENDLY	

TOTAL NUMBER OF CHECK MARKS	TOTAL NUMBER OF CHECK MARKS	TOTAL NUMBER OF CHECK MARKS	TOTAL NUMBER OF CHECK MARKS

Subtract column 3 from column 1 to get *A*. Subtract column 4 from column 2 to arrive at *B*. Your A total should be marked on the *vertical* line running up and down the center of the personality graph on the next page. Mark your B total on the *horizonal* line of the graph. Connect the dots to determine your basic personality.

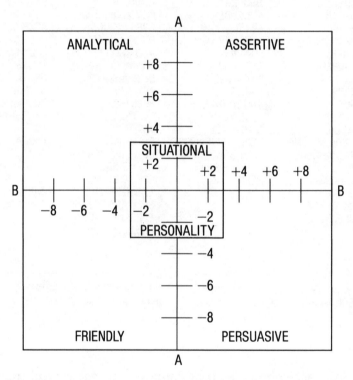

The quadrant in which your A total and B total intersect defines your basic personality type. See the following examples.

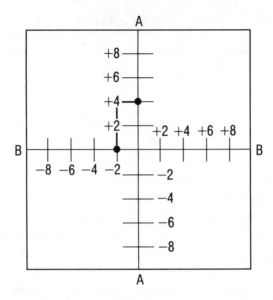

Example: Vertical number is +4. Horizontal number is −2. Basic personality is Analytical.

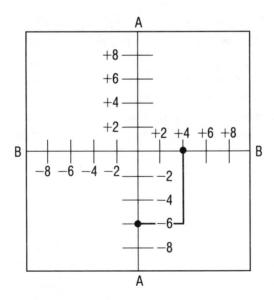

Example: Vertical number is −6. Horizontal number is +4. Basic personality is Persuasive.

THE FRIENDLY PERSONALITY

If you have a basic Friendly personality, you place a high value on friendship. You may close a high percentage of sales by doing favors for people. You probably invite clients to dinner and may be found fishing or at a baseball game with customers. Your personality will help you sell to other amiable people and to other individuals in need of friends. Socially inept Analytical people may respond favorably to your attentive personality.

One potential problem with the Friendly personality is that you may have a tendency to spend too much time closing sales. Furthermore, Assertive people with driving personalities will resent you if you waste their valuable time with idle conversation. The Persuasive personality will resent your lackadaisical attitude. The Analytical personality probably will prefer that you stick to the facts and not concern yourself with his or her personal considerations.

Never lose sight of your objective. Your primary purpose for meeting with people is to sell your company, your products or services, and yourself. This can best be accomplished by respecting everyone's time constraints, including your own. Place time limits on each appointment. Restrict the time allotted to make your presentations and don't run over. Whenever possible, book your appointments close together geographically and timewise. This will force you to minimize the time you spend in front of the customer. Make your presentations concise, factual, and persuasive. Close the sale and then leave.

I have seen many Friendly salespeople talk themselves out of a sale. If the prospect says, "Yes, I will take it," get the purchase order approved, pick up the check (if applicable), and leave! Anything you say after the moment the "buy decision" is made can have a negative impact on the end result.

If you are selling to a prospect with a Friendly personality, spend a little time discussing his or her personal interests, but keep the sales presentation on course. The Friendly personality may not want to share hard realities with you, but probe intensely and try to determine his or her ability to buy. To boost your ego and your hopes of landing an order, the Friendly personality actually may pretend to have authority that he or she does not have. This type of person simply would like to avoid disappointing anybody. Be polite, but be direct. (See Chapter 10, "Probing Made Easy.")

THE ASSERTIVE PERSONALITY

If you have a basic Assertive personality, you are task oriented and may judge yourself by your ability to get things accomplished. You set high goals for yourself and often achieve them within a reasonable time frame. You generally display a great amount of creativity in accomplishing your goals. You most likely are driven and hardworking and love a challenge. Assertive people make excellent salespeople because they usually are very enthusiastic about what they do. They tend to be well organized and, as a rule, do not waste time.

Assertive types make great sales managers because they impose the same results-oriented challenges they love on their subordinates. Management usually loves them because they get the job done, and they get it done on time. Most companies look for Assertive salespeople to open new markets because they can quickly scan the territory to find the most immediate business base. Once the market share is reached, however, the truly Assertive salesperson may become bored as the job begins to require more sales-account maintenance and less new-sales penetration. The smart management team will keep the Assertive salesperson challenged with new product introductions and/or new territories to conquer.

As with each personality type, there are negatives associated with the Assertive personality. These types tend to lose interest in a job rapidly and may change jobs frequently as they search for the next great challenge. They may be so anxious to close a sale and get the prospect's approval that they may exaggerate the truth or forget to mention the *problematic* aspects of the deal.

I've known Assertive personality types who have generated false call reports, charged personal expenses on their corporate accounts, and generated false purchase orders. Certainly, not all Assertive salespeople do these things, and it's impossible to paint a personality type with only one brush stroke. In my thirty years of selling and working with thousands of sales professionals, however, I have found that Assertive salespeople create the most headaches for sales management.

If you have a basic Assertive personality, you can improve your sales record by slowing down your sales presentations. Develop some empathy for your prospect. Try to see yourself, your company, and your products through your prospect's eyes. Remember that different people need different things, and if you intend to sell them something, you must fulfill those needs. For example, do not be so quick to accept a "no" from an Analytical personality. The Analytical type will not be impressed with your bravado, competence, and the ability to ask for the order before saying "hello." Another Assertive or a Persuasive personality will love you, but you probably will lose the Analytical and Friendly personalities. The Analytical type will suspect that you are hiding something, and the Friendly personality will think that you do not like him or her. Slow down, take a little extra time, and walk the Analytical prospect through the reasons why he or she is better off with *your* widget than with someone else's widget. Stop and ask for the Friendly prospect's opinions and thoughts as you proceed through the presentation.

If you are selling to an Assertive personality, always maintain good eye contact. When you first meet the Assertive personality, shake his hand with conviction. Make your product presentation concise, direct, and to the point. Be innovative and creative. Remember that your prospect is task oriented and wants to get the job done. Find out what he wants, show him how he can accomplish his goals in a short time frame, and you probably will sell him every time.

THE ANALYTICAL PERSONALITY

If you are blessed with an Analytical personality, you are less susceptible to the major mood swings often experienced by the other personalities. You tend to look at issues and decisions in a pragmatic manner. Because you generally view things in black-and-white terms, you are less likely than other personality types to make decisions based on instinct, gut feelings, or the advice of your local guru. You tend to be a conservative dresser and seldom offend anyone. Your sales presentations are fact based, direct, and to the point. Any statements you make usually are well documented. You enjoy intellectual pursuits and probably performed well on tests in school. You are reliable and steadfast and accept accountability for your actions. You tend to be trustworthy and well organized, and you usually do not object to filling out call reports, expense reports, and other required paperwork.

Unfortunately, you may get bogged down in details. Your presentations may be boring because you resort to providing a wealth of facts to convince your prospect to buy. Although facts are helpful, they frequently have little to do with why people buy something. The smart Analytical salesperson will develop a comprehensive, exciting presentation that incorporates the benefits of owning her product or using her service.

Every once in a while, wear a flamboyant tie or more trendy dress than you usually wear. Force yourself to be a little colorful, more exciting, and charismatic. Learn a few jokes to bring into play in a presentation when appropriate. Speak with enthusiasm and conviction. Get excited about your product! Loosen up and enjoy your sales job, your customers, and the challenge of making your product or service the most exciting in the world.

I know an Analytical saleswoman with fire and brimstone in her eyes who sold Bibles in church vestibules after religious services on Sunday. She would explain to prospects that a carpenter could not build a house without a hammer and the prospect would agree. Then she would ask the $1-million question: How can you teach the word of God in your home without the Bible? She then asked for the order and agreed to cover financing if the prospect bought a Bible immediately. She even persuaded people to buy Bibles for families who could not afford them. This Analytical saleswoman sold more than 100,000 Bibles a year, at a $4 profit per Bible, simply by compelling the sale. (See Chapter 15, "The Ten Best Closing Techniques.")

If you are selling to an Analytical personality, present all the factual reasons why your product should be purchased. Then present three or four reasons why your product should not be purchased, because you know that the Analytical mind already will be thinking about the reasons why he or she should not buy. Refrain from flamboyant, cavalier, and nonfactual presentations.

Opposites may attract in physics, but not so in the human arena. People tend to buy from people most like themselves. This is especially true when it comes to the Analytical personality. Dress conservatively and be prepared to back up everything you claim. If you claim that the Hilton Hotel chain is using your software program, present a testimonial letter from a Hilton Hotel manager. If you claim your product is the least expensive of its kind, use a comparative price chart to illustrate this fact. Assume that the Analytical prospect disbelieves everything you say, whether he does or does not.

THE PERSUASIVE PERSONALITY

If you were blessed with a basic Persuasive personality, you probably are accustomed to commanding attention through your excellent ability to communicate. Up-to-date on current events, Persuasive types are well read and articulate and are experts at creating word pictures. Extroverted, this personality type meets people easily and frequently is the life of the party. Billy Graham and Ronald Reagan have Persuasive personalities, as did John Kennedy. They make great public speakers, teachers, political leaders, and salespeople.

Knowing when to listen frequently will make the difference between closing the sale and leaving empty-handed. Unfortunately, Persuasive types may appear to some as know-it-alls, self-centered, and poor listeners. The Persuasive personality has this undying need to know everything. He reads every magazine that he can put his hands on. He watches documentaries on television and reads the newspaper from front to back. Simply stated, he has an insatiable need to know because knowledge enables him to gain respect and fit in anywhere. Sometimes the Persuasive personality will fabricate facts to dramatize a point or impress others. During one seminar experiment, I sepa-

rated the sales professionals into groups by personality
type. Each group comprised four people. I asked the first
person in each group to read a paragraph from my book,
How to Get Rich.

The paragraph described an entrepreneur who amassed
a fortune worth tens of millions of dollars by developing a
unique real estate development concept. The first person in
each group read the paragraph and then returned the book
to me. Each person who read the paragraph then was
asked to whisper the content to the next person, who
would whisper it to the next, until all four in each group
knew the content of the paragraph.

The purpose of the experiment was to demonstrate the
need to speak firsthand to the decision maker in a sales
situation and not rely on someone else to tell your sales
story. More important, the experiment illustrated the un-
canny ability of the Persuasive personality to commit facts
and information in general to memory. The group of Persuasive types was able to pass the information contained
in the paragraph verbally down the four-person line and
successfully come up with an understanding of the content
that was very close to the written word. The other groups
completely changed the story so that it was unrecogniza-
ble.

At another seminar, I excused ten Persuasive salespeople from the seminar room. When they returned, I asked
each of them five questions:

1. Why did you come to this seminar?
2. Do blonds have more fun?
3. Would you recognize Queen Tulare?
4. Who was the Green Bay Packers' quarterback in 1968?
5. How far is it from Los Angeles to Honolulu?

Only one of the ten Persuasive personality types stated that he would not recognize Queen Tulare. Actually, Queen Tulare was a fictitious person that I had created for the exercise. Each one of the ten supplied a name for the quarterback for the Green Bay Packers, and each one estimated the distance from Los Angeles to Honolulu. Few were right in these two questions, but all were emphatic about the accuracy of their answers. Persuasive personalities have a difficult time not knowing the answer to a question.

If you are a Persuasive type, remember that it's OK not to have an answer to every question! If you do not know the answer to a prospect's inquiry, simply say that you do not know and assure him or her that you will get the answer. Be careful not to rush your product presentations. You must remember that your prospect does not have the wealth of information that you have. You can't assume that the prospect has any prior knowledge about you, your company, or its products unless you've asked. Walk him or her through these areas slowly and methodically.

If you are selling to Persuasive personalities, you are in luck because these will be the easiest sales you will make. Give someone with a Persuasive personality ten reasons why he or she should buy your product. Pause, and then ask to be reminded of the points you've covered. Like magic, the Persuasive type will repeat the ten points with the same enthusiasm, punctuation, and delivery style. And after repeating what you said, the Persuasive person will have sold himself or herself on your product. If he or she has the financial capability, the prospect will find the purchase nearly irresistible. More professional salespeople have employed this singular sales technique than probably any other technique that I will discuss in this book.

THE SITUATIONAL PERSONALITY

If you found yourself in this rectangular area of the personality graph, you have many of the positive attributes characteristic of the other four personality types. You probably have some crossover negative personality traits as well. A Situational personality is very flexible. He or she can be very Assertive, Persuasive, extremely Friendly, or Analytical when necessary. Few people have a true Situational personality. Adolf Hitler had a Situational personality, as did Richard Burton and Clark Gable.

While Situational personalities are versatile, intriguing, and generally very popular, they can be moody and unpredictable, fickle to a fault, and difficult to work with. They are seldom satisfied, because what satisfies one aspect of their mixed personality usually conflicts with another aspect. The Assertive personality wants results yesterday, while the Analytical personality wants to take a more conservative approach, recognizing that a quick reaction may not ultimately produce the desired results. Such inner conflict may cause emotional problems and career conflicts for Situational personality types. But I suspect that Situational personalities occupy great positions of trust and influence. They are versatile and intellectually balanced, and they possess tremendous leadership skills for virtually everyone that comes in contact with them relates to them.

If you are selling to a Situational personality, your task is relatively easy because your prospect will relate to you on some level no matter what your personality is. One word of caution, however. Get a commitment as fast as you can because the Situational personality often will change his or her mind.

THE SALES DETECTIVE'S CHART TO PERSONALITY ASSESSMENT

THE FRIENDLY PERSONALITY

Attributes

Conservative dresser
Standard office grouping in
   warm colors
Photos of family and friends
   on desk and walls
Organization lapel pins
Will offer refreshments
Overly protective secretary
Will inquire about you with
   interest

Warm handshake
Good eye contact
Not time-conscious
Smiles easily
Team player
Always on time
Open body language
Patient
Stable demeanor
Nonoffensive mannerisms

Key Words

Love	Belonging	Couple	New
Friendship	Regain	We	Worth
Together	Aware	Ingratiate	Share
Us	Strong	Join	Special
Partnership	Embrace	Encourage	

THE ASSERTIVE PERSONALITY

Attributes

Poorly organized/messy desk
Pictures of cars, boats,
   predatory animals on walls
Interrupts frequently
Self-confident
Poor listener
Maverick, loner
Impatient
Stylish, colorful dresser
Bold office furnishings
Especially well groomed/
   manicured nails/shined
   shoes
Inconsistent eye contact

Strong, quick handshake
Always late for appointments
Likes fast, expensive cars
Brash at times
Self-indulgent
Optimistic
Flamboyant
Speaks quickly
Likes contact sports
Charismatic
Fun to be around

Key Words

Money	Strong	Work	Manage
Be	Control	Obtain	Strike
Power	Bold	Commerce	Rich
Life	Wealth	Run	Own
Mine	Me	Roar	Get
Activate	Action	Health	

THE ANALYTICAL PERSONALITY

Attributes

Conservative dresser
Conservative office furnishings
Prefers light, pastel colors
Weak, very slow handshake
Keeps appointments
Slow to make a decision
Does not make rash promises
Well groomed
Messy desk
Good eye contact
Patient

Deliberate
Good time manager
Drives standard car
Does not like to eat out
Reliable parent and spouse
Likes visiting museums and
   art galleries
Boring
Enjoys the arts
Good listener
Relies heavily on facts

Key Words

Numbers	Finance	Prosper	Corroborative
Math	Accountable	Accurate	Proof
Structure	Fiduciary	Teach	Substantiate
Balance	Control	Instruct	
Charge	Save	Learn	

THE PERSUASIVE PERSONALITY

Attributes

Stylish dresser
Good color coordination in
  wide range of colors
Wears feelings on his or her
  sleeve
Articulates very well
Shakes hands firmly with
  interest
Loves television
  documentaries
Very opinionated
Intellectual
Interested in modern art
Life of the party

Changes subject frequently
Likes jewelry
Good eye contact
Contemporary office
  furnishings
Good communicator
Excellent listener
Reads incessantly
Moody
Pictures of wildlife,
  landscapes, family in office
Likes to do several things at
  once

Key Words

Learn	Issue	Excite	Colorful
Travel	Beauty	Meaning	Challenge
Spontaneous	Perpetuate	Strike	Win
Life	Absorb	Formidable	Glamorous
Earn	Fulfill	Versatile	Flexible

THE SITUATIONAL PERSONALITY

Attributes

Moderate dresser
Expensive tastes
Wide range of interests
Usually on time to meetings
Friendly yet aloof
Poor eye contact
Disengages handshake quickly
Demands much
Poor sense of humor
Wide range of religious beliefs
Addictions could be a problem
Very high-strung

Prefers neutral colors
Enjoys good restaurants
Likes sports, the arts
Excellent team player
Spontaneous
Frequently angry
Poor public speaker
Opinionated
Gives little
Usually in a hurry
Can be very moody
Very impatient

Key Words

Peaceful	Result	Middle	Moderate
Life	Grant	License	Permit
Judgment	Struck	Variety	Keep
Paid	Quick	Health	Food
Passage	Quiet	God	Allow
Flexible	Versatile	Start	

Well, there you have it. If you want to sell, you have to sell to people. How your personality interrelates with your prospect's personality ultimately will determine whether or not you get the order, the size of the order, and how long you will be able to keep out your competitors. Begin assessing everyone's personality, from your spouse and children to your coworkers. Most important, start to assess each and every prospect's personality *before* making your presentation, if possible.

Once you ascertain your prospect's personality type, you will be able to address his or her conscious concerns and unconscious needs. The first two questions I ask myself on each and every sales call are: 1) Is the prospect *qualified* to buy my product? In other words, does the prospect have the money and the authority to buy? 2) What is the prospect's personality? The answer to the second question will tell me how best to approach the prospect and what closing technique to employ. (See Chapter 15, "The Ten Best Closing Techniques," and Chapter 16, "Five'll Get You Ten.")

As in all things, there are exceptions to every rule, and the Sales Detective Personality Chart is not foolproof. You may find a Friendly personality who likes contact sports or a Situational personality who is not spontaneous. All in all, though, I think you will find that the personality traits are fairly consistent and, therefore, usually predictable.

Being able to assess your prospect's personality accurately also will help you a great deal whenever you decide to use Neuro-Linguistic Programming, which I hope will be on every sales call you make after reading Chapter 5, "Win with Neuro-Linguistic Programming."

WORK ASSIGNMENT

1. Write sales letters thanking a Friendly personality, an Analytical personality, a Persuasive personality, an Assertive personality, and a Situational personality for allowing you the opportunity to make a sales presentation. In the letters, use as many of the key words of each personality as possible.

Remember to draft all of your future sales letters based on each customer's personality. Incorporate the key words into your presentations and into all verbal and written communications.

2. On a piece of paper, list ten people you know and identify each of their personalities.

5
Win with Neuro-Linguistic Programming

"Trumpet in a herd of elephants; crow in the company of cocks; bleat in a flock of sheep."
—Malayan Proverb

Science Digest described Neuro-Linguistic Programming (NLP) as "the most important synthesis of knowledge about human communications" since the humanistic psychology movement of the 1960s. The origins of NLP usually are traced to California in the 1970s and mathematician Richard Bandler and linguist John Grinder. Anthony Robbins has popularized NLP in his personal power training seminars. Robbins used fire-walking exercises to demonstrate that the impossible is possible and that people can eliminate the fears that keep them from attaining their goals.

NLP DEFINED

Basically, NLP is concerned with how individuals interpret and understand the world. NLP has been defined as the science of how to program the mind, and its critics call it

manipulative. Robbins defines NLP as the science of discovering the consistent, logical action patterns of excellence and duplicating them. If one person can do something, so can anyone else by duplicating (modeling) the
same mental and physical actions. Modeling is discovering
how someone produces a particular desired result and then
programming one's mind and body to duplicate that result.

Bandler and Grinder boasted that they could change
behavior—even eliminate phobias—quickly and pain-
lessly. Unlike traditional psychology, NLP does not deal
with the "why" of a behavior but with the "how." NLP
trainers use a variety of techniques to help individuals
change their lives. Robbins discusses how behavior is
determined by a person's physiology (how one uses one's
body) and by a person's internal representations (how one
represents things in one's mind). Simply changing either of
these two can change one's behavior. For instance, if you
adopt a posture associated with being bored and tired, you
probably would be looking downward, your shoulders
would be hunched over, your facial muscles might sag,
and your breathing might be shallow. If you change your
physiology by sitting upright, breathing deeply, looking
forward, and smiling, your *emotional* state also will
change.

Every individual selects how he or she perceives the
world. Bandler taught his students that by taking control
of the way they represent input to their brains, they actually can change the way they experience life. Robbins
teaches a "scramble" technique to change how an individual feels about something. He first asks trainees to remember an upsetting experience involving another individual. Then he asks each student to alter that image by
imagining the individual in a ridiculous manner, such as
wearing a clown suit and a bulbous red nose. Robbins then
asks each trainee to run the "movie" of the upsetting event

backwards, complete with the individual in a clown suit. Now the upsetting experience has been replaced with one that's comical, and that's how each trainee will remember it.

Winners are optimistic, not pessimistic. Dr. Martin E. P. Seligman of the University of Pennsylvania, Philadelphia, reports that to become an optimist, you must change *the way you explain life events to yourself.* To do this, you must develop new ways to "talk" to yourself. To become more persistent, a trait required for successful selling, you just need to change your explanatory style.

According to NLP theory, each of us favors one of three modes of perceiving the world: through visuals, sounds, or emotions/feelings (kinesthetically). Because one of the goals of NLP training is better communication, Bandler's training sessions showed participants how to identify which of the three modes an individual prefers by studying his or her eye movements, rate of breathing, and other body signals. Once an individual's style is identified, others can speak to him in his specific "language."

Proponents of NLP believe that effective communication is accomplished largely through a technique called "pacing." To establish rapport, advocates suggest a subtle matching and mirroring (using the mirror image) of a person's natural rhythms (such as respiration), body language (eye movements, facial expressions, arm and leg movements, for example), and voice (tone, tempo, volume). This concept is based on a 1967 UCLA study that found that 55 percent of what people respond to happens *visually*, while 38 percent of our responses are sound based. A mere 7 percent of all responses are based on the words actually used (*The Atlantic Monthly*, October 1989).

Advertising agencies such as Warwick, Baker & Fiore have incorporated NLP techniques into their consumer research. Corporations such as AT&T, Chase Manhattan, and Coca-Cola have begun to study NLP as a communications and negotiating tool, according to *Adweek* (Western edition, October 15, 1990). If this new "science" worked as well as Bandler said it did, could people be manipulated to do exactly as others wanted them to do?

THE SKEPTICS RESPOND

NLP was viewed as revolutionary for it claimed to give the therapist—not the client—the power of change. Even though NLP is embraced by some psychotherapists and educators, certain skeptics have challenged its theories and asked for evidence of its claims of almost miraculous change. Bandler and Grinder argued that because they were not scientists, they were not required to prove anything. While professionals doubted and questioned its basic tenets, NLP has continued to fascinate the lay public.

Bandler was tried and acquitted for the 1986 murder of Corine Christensen, an NLP student and fellow cocaine user. Christensen had been shot with Bandler's gun during a visit from Bandler and Christensen's former boyfriend. Bandler and Grinder had once written, "Everyone ought to have several histories" (*Mother Jones*, February/March 1989), and apparently Bandler cultivated a legendary personal history. According to some observers, he had become lost in his abilities to imitate and manipulate, and he assumed different identities and fabricated stories about himself. Despite Bandler's personal history, he and Grinder developed some interesting techniques in the area of human persuasion.

LIKES ATTRACT

Humans are pretty predictable creatures. When we get burned, our reactions are all similar. We jerk away from the source of fire, usually even before our brains have registered the pain. In this case, our reaction is an automatic, involuntary one. Wouldn't it be wonderful if you could get a prospect to automatically respond to you? You say or do something in particular, and she automatically gives you a purchase order. That's a pretty wonderful concept, don't you think?

People buy from people who are most like themselves. Although in physics, opposites attract and likes repel, in sales, *likes attract.* It's been proven that people are most comfortable with someone like themselves. Think about this concept for a moment: *People are more responsive to those who are similar to themselves.* Do you feel most at ease when you are around others who are like you? You know what makes you tick. You trust your own judgment. It follows that you would understand and trust others like yourself.

Step into your prospect's shoes, consciously become as much like your prospect as possible, and he will instinctively trust you. Use pacing and mirror your prospect. Tap your finger within his eyesight in rhythm with his breathing. If he speaks slowly, adjust the speed of your speech accordingly. If he crosses his legs, after a short delay, cross your legs. Neuro-Linguistic Programming is not a game of Simon Says, so be careful not to offend your prospect. A Texan might take offense at a native New Yorker trying to mimic his drawl and vice versa.

By mirroring the prospect and gaining her trust, your chances of closing the sale are significantly improved. Assuming the same posture sends messages back to the other person, and the probability is that he or she will behave in a responsive manner. If a prospect studies your documentation with great interest, show great interest in the documentation. If she leans forward toward you, adjust your position in the chair and lean toward her. Get inside your prospect's head. See through her eyes, hear through her ears, and speak using her voice, and the chances are outstanding that she will order your product.

NLP IN PRACTICE

Does this sound pretty complex? Let's walk through a real-life type of sales call where NLP techniques are put into play. For the purpose of this illustration, I will concentrate only on the Neuro-Linguistic Programming elements and not on the actual elements of the sales call.

From my previous discussions with Ted Smith, I've learned that he is an amiable person with a great deal of authority. In short, this friendly fellow can buy what I am selling. He probably is around sixty years old, self-made, and has a reputation for being strong-minded but fair. Integrity means a great deal to Ted. In this hypothetical situation, let's assume that I am selling infomercial production services to motivational speakers who never have used television to sell their books, audiotapes, videotapes, and tickets to their seminars.

When I arrive in the city where Ted resides, I will meet him for dinner at my hotel. I want him to know that I'd like to join him in a more relaxed atmosphere away from the normal surroundings where he may be distracted. I want him to drive to meet me so that he feels like he is making a contribution to the success of the meeting. I've invited his wife to join us.

When Ted arrives, I notice that he is wearing a brown suit, white shirt, stylish tie, a Knights of Columbus lapel pin, and a college ring on his right hand. His handshake is firm, and so is mine. The eye contact between us is good. Ted starts almost every sentence with "Chuck," so I respond similarly by beginning almost every sentence using his or his wife's name. Because he doesn't order an alco-

holic drink, neither do I. When Ted orders fish with aspar-
agus, I ask the waiter to double the order.

I ask Ted if being a Catholic and a native New Yorker
has had an adverse impact on his business in Texas. He
responds in the negative, citing examples of kindness
shown to him since he moved to Dallas. I, in turn, remi-
nisce about the time I volunteered the membership of my
local Jaycees Club to paint the neighborhood's Catholic
church, which I thought would be a perfect spot for our
annual membership dance. Then I committed an unforgiv-
able sin. After volunteering the members' painting services, I failed to show up the night of the painting because
I was out of town on business. It was almost six months
before some of the members started talking to me again! I
can tell that Ed appreciates my sense of humor and amiable attitude.

As our dinner progresses, I am able to study Ted's style
and mannerisms. Because he speaks quietly and slowly, I
adjust my speech accordingly. I notice that he eats slowly,
so I take my time and enjoy my meal. When Ted laughs, I
laugh and try to imitate his laughter. When he mentions a
personal experience, I listen intently and then relay a
similar personal story.

I ask Ted what his thoughts are about infomercials, and
he admits that he is impressed with the impact that infomercials have on viewing audiences. Because I know that
he likes the concept of infomercials and his body language
shows me that he trusts me, I simply "assume" the sale: I
suggest that his infomercial be produced the following
month. He agrees and the sale is finalized.

Neuro-Linguistic Programming is indeed a useful sales
tool. It is not a secret weapon. You cannot take the deci-
sion-making process away from your prospect by casting
a hypnotic spell or compelling him to sign your sales
agreement. It is not a manipulative tool to get the woman
of your dreams to say "yes" to your marital proposal, nor

can you use it to get out of a traffic ticket. You *can* use it to develop strong rapport and experience deeper communication in your interpersonal relationships.

If you don't have the benefit of a face-to-face meeting, attempt to mirror your prospect's speech patterns on the telephone without being too obvious. If she speaks rapidly, you speak rapidly also. Emulate her diction. Use some of the same expressions and articulate your words in a similar fashion. To connote empathy and enhance the mirroring effect, scatter the following words throughout your conversation: *us, we, you, our, together, jointly.*

NLP IN A GROUP SETTING

What do you do when making a presentation to a group? First, find out what the group's objectives are and who is in power if you don't already know this prior to the meeting. You should know after only a few moments who is in control by the assertive actions or leadership role he or she takes. Mirror the group *leader.* In all likelihood, the other members of the group respect this person for the power he or she wields, if nothing else. If you adopt the leader's style, the group will respond to you as they do to their leader.

If the group is strong and committed and displays a cohesive, common agenda, then jump right in and become a member of the group: "With *our* program *we* can enjoy a 30 percent increase in productivity by the end of the month." Such a statement shows that you are a member of the same team, trying to score a home run for the team as much as for yourself.

YOUR CLOTHES COMMUNICATE

When I know I am making a sales presentation to a conservative banker, accountant, or businessperson, I wear my pin-striped suit, a conservative tie, and wing tip shoes. I never wear a fraternal organization pin, because Masons sometimes do not like Knights of Columbus, just as a staunch Democrat might get upset with a vocal Republican in his or her midst. If you are going to wear a lapel pin, wear one that anyone might wear, such as a Rotary, Jaycees, Optimist Club, or Toastmasters pin. If I had a ten-year pin from my company, I would wear that because it tells the prospect that I am a stable performer.

Each day before you get dressed, think about the people you are going to call on and dress appropriately. Take your cues from your customers. Don't dress flamboyantly if you intend to call on bankers, stockbrokers, investment bankers, or executives. Wearing a conservative three-piece suit when calling on fashion designers, ad agency art directors, or theatrical customers probably will impress no ·one. If you have problems coordinating clothing as I do, and there is no one in your office whose advice you trust, consider hiring a wardrobe consultant. It may cost you a few hundred dollars, but in the long run, the investment should pay off in increased commissions!

WORK ASSIGNMENT

Practice "pacing" techniques on at least *five* prospects this week. Select prospects with whom you've had little previous contact or with whom you've had no personal relationship. At first, it may seem a little strange, but the more you integrate NLP into your sales routine, the more you'll benefit. Afterward, think about the encounter. Did you feel closer to the person? Were you more in control of the meeting. Did the prospect notice anything? Was there an improvement in communication?

6
Masterful Marketing

"My decision is maybe, and that's final."

—Unknown

You could be well on your way to becoming one of the world's top salespersons, you could become an expert in assessing personalities, and you might even be able to develop your NLP skills to a fine art. This is all worthless, however, if you don't sell to the *right* market. You cannot sell a Lear jet to a car mechanic (unless, of course, he has just won the lottery). You cannot sell oil investments to factory workers or bikinis to residents of the North Pole. No matter how good you are, you must first identify your market and fully understand it before you can sell to it.

MARKET DEFINED

Let's first define what a market is. A market is that group of people who need and desire a product or service more than any other group of people *and* who have the ability to acquire and use that product or service.

YOUR PLACE IN THE MARKET

The marketplace is the arena where every business enterprise is finally judged a winner or a loser. It is where you and your competitors meet head-on to convince the buyer—the customer—to choose one of you over the other and where your efforts finally will be pronounced successful or unsuccessful.

Companies do not make mistakes. People make mistakes. Too many mistakes, of course, can cause lasting damage—even failure—in the marketplace, for the marketplace is made up of people. People perceive things, draw conclusions, remember things. Companies can face years of expensive rebuilding for mistakes that have been widely publicized. In some cases, companies pay for the actions of others, actions completely beyond their immediate control. Consider, for example, the tampering of Tylenol capsules that led to deaths in the mid-1980s. Fear in the marketplace could have destroyed the company.

Every member of the company team either helps or hinders the company—there is no neutral ground. If the finance department has too many people on staff, it drives up overhead, making competitive pricing even more difficult when potential buyers are already sensitive to price. If the personnel department ineffectively screens candidates and places the wrong people in customer service, the results are both unhappy employees and customers. Each management function must have something to do with the relationship between the company and the marketplace, or the function should not exist in the company.

When you decide to become a member of a sales team, you accept the responsibility of helping your company win in the marketplace. There is no other arena, and there is no desirable alternative to winning.

WHY DO PEOPLE BUY?

When making the decision to buy, people take a number of factors into consideration. Some of the more noteworthy are:

- *Need* for the product or service. A car must be replaced when worn out (a product need). A car must be repaired when broken (a service need).
- *Desire* for the product or service. Some things people simply want, as opposed to need. Eating is a need, but going to a restaurant for dinner is a desire. When a specific restaurant is selected, the "buy decision" has been made.
- *Price.* Assuming that a comparable level of quality exists among products or services, people generally will look for a lower price. A company that charges higher prices than its competitors must convince potential buyers that its product is superior in terms of quality, features, and perceived value to the buyer, or that it is more convenient to acquire.
- *Quality.* The degree of excellence of a product or service. Although the forms and levels of product or service quality differ widely, people generally expect more when they pay more.
- *Value.* Though value is difficult to define precisely, people have some minimum expectation of value when they buy anything. An inexpensive pen that skips frequently does not meet the minimum expectation of value. Neither does a rude bank teller.

  Companies with reputations for poor quality or service run much greater risks than companies that charge more for products or services. Neiman Marcus, for example, is recognized for the high quality of its products and services. People expect to pay more, but they expect a greater value when they shop at a Neiman Marcus store.
- *Convenience.* This term also takes many forms. For example, convenience may be how close the supermarket is to home. Or it may be weekend plumbing service. Long waiting lines may make a bank or grocery store inconvenient even though the customer may

have to drive only a few minutes to get there.

Convenience can be influenced by need. Patients obviously accept greater inconvenience to see the physicians of their choice than they would accept when deciding where to have their clothes cleaned.

Desire influences the buyer's view of convenience. A boating enthusiast may pass by several boat dealers to buy a specific product.

Price often influences the value that buyers associate with convenience. The growth of regional discount stores in recent years demonstrates buyer willingness to drive farther and wait in line longer to save money.

• *Risk.* If the potential buyer believes that the risk is too high, the purchase will not be made. Consider, for example, the reluctance of Americans to travel abroad when the threat of international terrorism is highly publicized. Regardless of the price, quality, or real value offered, many people will not buy. When there is a perceived risk of bank failure, depositors take their money elsewhere. Those threatened with unemployment frequently alter their buying habits dramatically. (The Panamanian war did not dissuade me from taking a transcanal cruise in 1989; it did dissuade others, apparently, because the ship was half-empty.)

These factors are constantly at work in the marketplace, as are other dynamics. People differ, and so do their attitudes concerning needs for products and services. Circumstances differ, altering the buying decisions people make. You will be a better salesperson if you thoroughly understand the nature of the marketplace that your company serves.

UNDERSTAND YOUR MARKET

Before hitting the telephones or the streets, ask yourself several basic questions:

- Who stands to gain the most from my product or service?
- Who is the decision maker?
- What are the submarkets?

Let's assume that you want to sell men's underwear. Traditionally, B.V.D.s have been a dominant force in the marketplace. (By the way, B.V.D. stands for Bradley, Voorheis, and Day, the last names of the men who organized the company.) You offer colored underwear in ten different styles, from bikini to athletic, and everything in between. Your total market is men and boys of all ages. Pretty obvious, right?

Wrong. Although men influence the brand chosen, *women* make up nearly 100 percent of the buyers of boys' underwear and about 70 percent of the buyers of men's underwear. Women like variety and are accustomed to buying colored underwear in different cuts and styles. They are receptive consumers. Advertisements and marketing efforts for men's underwear frequently are directed toward women. Although you may advertise in men's magazines, you must advertise in women's magazines, position your display racks near women's clothing departments, target your direct mail to women, and then watch your sales go up.

To be successful in any field, you first must understand your market and identify the decision makers, and only then can you start the sales process.

Smart marketers "seed" their markets by identifying

those key people whose actions or opinions can persuade or positively affect their potential buyers. The concept is that if you can get these individuals to try your product and they like it, the balance of the market will not be far behind.

One computer software company in New England has been successfully seeding its market for a software program for managers. As with other such software programs, there is a "breeder effect": Once one party starts using the program, others will follow. Using various lists he has purchased, the marketing director invites the targets to attend his seminars. After showing the seminar attendees how the program works, he gives each a free copy of the software and training manual. If the seminar leader has been successful, each attendee will fall in love with the program and will sell it to others in his or her office.

I eventually made millions of dollars by understanding my market. For almost two years, however, I beat my head against the proverbial wall trying to sell portable dialysis machines to kidney dialysis patients so they could travel and still clean their uremic-poisoned blood three times a week. At best, I'd sell an occasional machine here and there.

Just as I was about to give up my dialysis-equipment sales career, I took the time to really analyze my market. I decided that those who could benefit most from the traveling dialysis patient would be the cruise lines, hotels, or resorts. As if by magic, I began to sell hundreds of dialysis machines to these targets. Dialysis patients now could enjoy the convenience of having a treatment at no additional cost while enjoying their vacations.

What did I do? I simply analyzed the market carefully and determined the right method to sell my product to that specific market.

Once you determine your market, you usually can buy
lists of prospects from any number of list brokerage companies. If, for instance, you are selling burglar-alarm systems, you can buy lists of new home buyers. Generally, the
cost of a list will be $60 to $120 per thousand. The public
library is also a terrific resource for it has telephone books
from all over the country and other handy reference materials from which to get leads.

Selling Air

Trying to sell windmills to wealthy investors for $150,000
each, I again found myself beating my head against the
wall. (Please refer to Chapter 3, "The Cream of the Sales
Crop.") The U.S. government offered tax credits and accelerated depreciation to people who bought these incredible,
ten-story-high windmills. I talked to prospects with six-
and seven-figure incomes with hopes that I could sell them
a windmill. I would drive each prospect to the "windpark"
to show how the windmills worked and how substantially
the windmills were constructed. While everyone was truly
impressed, no one bought one!

After analyzing the political climate, federal regulations,
state laws, and general market trends, I decided to stop
selling the windmills directly to wealthy clients. Instead, I
started to believe that my weekly trips to the "windfarm,"
were a waste of time. During the years when the railroad
was a new, alternative form of transportation, the U.S.
government offered investors tax credits on railway investments as it now was offering tax credits on the windmills. I reasoned that because the railroad investors probably did not run out and kick the train rails, why would
potential wind-turbine investors need to see the windpark?

I began to call on financial planners and CPAs and

proposed that they form small investment groups called limited partnerships. I offered each financial planner or CPA a $30,000 fee for each wind turbine he sold to his clients. With this new program, the financial planners and CPAs closed millions of dollars in sales. That's understanding your market.

In other words, the financial planners and CPAs could give their clients major assets essentially *for free*. Each client's net worth went up; the government succeeded in producing alternative energy while reducing our dependence on foreign oil sources; precious fossil fuels were preserved for future generations; and the financial planners and CPAs made lots of money.

I made millions of dollars in commissions once I identified and targeted my real markets. You, too, can break apart from the crowd by thoroughly analyzing your market.

Identify Your Real Customers

If the greatest salesperson in the world is selling to the wrong market, she is doomed to fail. Imagine a diaper-service sales representative selling to adults without children, a Bible salesperson selling to a community of atheists, an ice cream salesperson selling to weight-loss centers, or a wheelchair sales representative selling to healthy college athletes.

Of course, these are extreme examples, and you would be right in arguing that the likelihood of an ice cream salesperson attempting to sell to weight-loss centers is pretty remote. I have used these extreme examples to illustrate my point. If you are selling to the wrong person, you are not going to close a sale. Just imagine the greatest Bible salesperson in the world trying to convince an atheist to buy a Bible. He may sell one Bible on a rare occasion, and he may even convert an occasional sinner, but imagine the effort required! Compare the sales effort required if the same salesperson sold to religious fraternal organizations, frequent churchgoers, and Bible study groups. In short, you must know your audience and its buying motives.

Once you decide who your customers are, you must determine who the decision makers are. Recently, I met a salesperson who sold a unique product to the airlines. Her seat-mounted closed-circuit video monitor enables each passenger to select one of twenty movies that he or she would like to see. The passenger pays $5 to the flight attendant who remotely turns on the individual monitor, allowing each person to see the movie of his or her choice.

The deregulated airline industry has to be more competitive than ever. Each airline continually tries to outdo the others. Price wars and frequent-mileage bonus programs are commonplace. This ever-increasing competitive atmosphere is forcing airlines to improve service and find additional profits wherever they can, which is a pretty tall order when you think about it. Better service translates into more personnel at the ticket counters, on the reservations lines, and in the airplane cabins. That means increased overhead.

This bright salesperson asked herself two key questions: Who has the most to win or lose if passengers select one airline over another? Who has the most to win or lose if revenue and profit are increased or decreased? Both questions had the same answer: the president of the airline. The salesperson made appointments only with presidents to sell her closed-circuit video monitor systems. She agreed to give one major carrier a one-year exclusive to distinguish itself from its competitors. The carrier had so many airplanes that 100 percent of the salesperson's initial production was sold with her first commitment.

Sure, you may be one of those extraordinary sellers who

can sell bikinis to Eskimos, but why try? I would rather
see you sell more swimming suits to Tahitians or Ha-
waiians. Package two suits together; sell his-and-hers
matching sets or combination swimming suit/short sets;
install bathing-suit vending machines; enlist banks to give
away swimwear with the opening of new accounts; ask
waitresses to wear your swimwear while serving customers; get bars or lounges to hold bathing-suit contests, and
you provide the prizes (swimwear, of course). Make a deal
with the suntan-lotion manufacturers and/or distributors
to give a $1 discount with proof of a bathing-suit pur-
chase. Get the local television stations to talk about your
swimwear promotions on the news. The marketing ideas
are endless. Doesn't this sound more exciting than whip-
ping a bunch of huskies into transporting you from Eskimo village to Eskimo village and making an idiot out of
yourself when you arrive?

I started a consumer magazine for heart patients in 1988.
My original business plan spelled out who the advertisers
were going to be. I reasoned that pharmaceutical manufacturers would want to advertise in a magazine that was
read by cardiac patients. I also enlisted heart-healthy food
manufacturers such as Promise margarine and Quaker
Oats. I sold ad space to exercise-equipment manufacturers,
travel agencies (because heart patients typically were
older with large disposable incomes), nursing homes, specialty hospitals, psychiatric clinics specializing in stress
management, and medical alarm-system manufacturers.
Because my audience was older, I reasoned that there
could be submarkets in gardening supplies, eye care, dental care, prosthetics, ambulatory equipment (canes,
walkers, crutches, and wheelchairs), financial-investment
opportunities, money-management plans, and estate-plan-
ning consultants. Finally, I envisioned a classified section
for subscribers to advertise used medical equipment.

As it turned out, after almost two years, the only advertisers I had were heart-healthy food manufacturers. Pharmaceutical companies were prohibited from advertising prescription drugs. My readers purchased the bulk of their medical supplies from local medical-supply companies. I found that, by and large, heart patients were afraid to travel because many live with the ever-present fear of having a medical emergency. Frequently, their financial resources were limited, or they had invested their funds so that the interest income could supplement their Social Security payments. In short, I really did not know my market.

I decided to invite potential advertisers from each market segment to a dinner workshop. I offered $100 to each for his or her professional input. The results were amazing.

The general consensus was that the heart-healthy food advertisers already were reaching my heart-patient audience with their television, radio, newspaper, and general health-magazine advertising campaigns. These advertisers were reaching their audiences at an average cost of $8 per 1,000 viewers, listeners, and readers. I was charging more than $25 per 1,000 readers. Even though I had a niche market, it was pretty difficult to justify the cost to advertise in my magazine.

I learned that the ambulatory-equipment advertisers concentrated their advertising dollars in local distributor ad campaigns. A distributor would advertise in a local newspaper and the manufacturer paid half of the cost.

After taking careful notes, I had to face the reality of my advertising market: The heart-healthy food advertisers represented the group with the greatest advertising potential for my magazine. I concentrated my sales efforts in that market from that day forward. Once I attained a reasonable customer base in my primary market by lowering my ad page rate and increasing the volume of ads, then I could concentrate my sales efforts in secondary markets such as over-the-counter pharmaceuticals and the travel industry.

Workshop meetings, or focus groups as they are sometimes called, really work. Organize your own to help you identify your true customers and analyze your market more completely.

HOW DO YOU ANALYZE YOUR MARKET?

Key elements to analyze when assessing your market include your product or service; your customers; your competition; and industry, environmental, and market trends.

On a piece of paper, answer the following questions as they relate to your product or service. Remember that you aren't necessarily looking for the predictable answer, so don't just write down the first thought that automatically comes to mind. Give each of these questions some consideration and be thorough.

Product or Service

1. Describe the product or service you sell.
2. How is the product or service positioned?
3. How is the product or service priced?
4. How does your company promote the product or service?
5. How is your product or service distributed?
6. What are the major strengths of your product or service?
7. What are the major limitations of your product or service?

Customers

1. Who are your present and potential customers?
2. What are their needs?
3. Does your product or service adequately meet those needs? If not, how can you better meet your customers' needs?
4. What do your customers perceive as "value"?
5. Who are the decision makers?
6. How do your customers buy your product or service?

Competition

1. How is your industry structured?
2. Who are your present and potential competitors?
3. What are the competitors' strengths?
4. What are the competitors' weaknesses?
5. What are your company's competitive strengths?
6. What are your company's competitive limitations?
7. Does your company have a competitive advantage or market niche? If not, can it develop one?
8. What are some of the obstacles to market entry that your company faces? Price? Distribution? Geography?
9. Have the company's submarkets been clearly identified and defined?

Trends

1. Are there industry, market, and/or other trends (political, environmental, social) that are having or could have an impact on your sales?
2. What opportunities might these trends present?
3. What problems might arise as a result of the trends?

You should be well on your way to analyzing your market. Once you understand who your targets *really* are, then you can succeed in securing the volume of sales that you desire.

GOAL SETTING

You can't create a marketing plan until you've established your sales and marketing goals. Effective goal setting is fundamental to successful company performance and can be an extremely powerful tool in reaching sales targets. Goal setting can be accomplished with relative ease, provided that goals are interactively established and focused. There should be a dialogue between the manager and the staff concerning what the goals should be, and the goals should relate directly to the jobs being performed.

Goals are specific, measurable things that must be attained during a specified time period to achieve a particular objective. Goals should direct individuals, departments, or an organization toward a particular end. Goals should be clearly stated and realistic, and responsibility for these goals should be assigned to a specific individual or individuals. Otherwise, goal setting is a meaningless ritual, the results of which are wasted time, poor performance, and general frustration.

Action plans often are used in conjunction with goals and should specify the particular steps that must be performed to achieve the goal. Action plans do not outline something that is to be achieved or accomplished; instead, they are specific activities that are performed by one or more individuals as stepping-stones to reach a goal.

An example of a goal set by a printing-services salesperson and its corresponding action steps are as follows:

Goal: To pursue fifteen new key accounts and make formal presentations to each by March 31, 199__.
Action Step: To select the top five companies in the three

best markets and investigate their use of printing
services and their printing needs by June 1, 199__.

Action Step: To contact the key decision makers in the
fifteen companies and probe them about their specific needs by September 1, 199__.

Action Step: To complete outlines for presentations and
mock-up prospect-specific samples for each of the
fifteen prospects by January 15, 199__.

Action Step: To make presentations and review the outcome of each by March 31, 199__.

What number of goals should an individual be held
accountable for? The best answer is *not more than is
reasonable*. Otherwise, you run the risk of jeopardizing all
of them. Five to six is probably a good range to start.
Fewer than six may not "stretch" you, while more than six
probably will overwhelm you. Usually, several action
steps will be needed for each goal you set.

Whatever the reasonable number of goals turns out to
be, it also is important to remember that goal setting is an
event. The process of acting to reach goals will be con-
cluded, and the act of setting new goals will recur. The
cycle runs something like this:

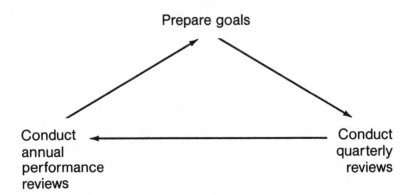

The process begins with the employee and the manager jointly establishing goals. Although agreement of a mutually acceptable level of accomplishment between the person setting the goal and his or her manager is critical, remember that the person setting the goal is *you*, not the boss.

The goals should be attainable and should call for improved performance. Progress toward these goals should be reviewed regularly—at least quarterly. Regular progress reviews provide the structure for feedback between sales manager and salesperson, and allow for an opportunity to adjust or change goals, if necessary. Review periods also involve self-analysis on the progress made. Don't confuse activity with accomplishment. Make sure that progress actually has occurred.

The annual (or semiannual) performance review will contain no surprises to the employee if regular progress reviews have occurred. Poor performance in reaching goals may be a reflection on the sales manager if he or she fails to use the regular reviews as opportunities to redirect an employee's behavior. It is important to note that for goal setting to be successful, each phase of the activity must be driven by purpose.

Personal goals may be included with business goals. A personal goal, such as continuing one's education or becoming a member of an association, helps humanize the relationship between a sales manager and a salesperson. Accomplishing personal goals also may improve an individual's self-esteem.

It must be emphasized that responsibility, authority, and accountability go hand in hand with goal setting. If you cannot accept these, don't bother to set goals.

Whatever your career, your effectiveness at setting and meeting goals could be the impetus to get you where you want to be in terms of personal and professional performance level. As part of a companywide performance appraisal program, goal setting has the potential to be a tremendous organizational propellant.

WORK ASSIGNMENT

On a piece of paper, write down five to six professional goals and the appropriate action steps that you must take to achieve these goals.

7
Care for Some H$_2$O, or Would You Prefer Delicious, Cool, Clear, Pure Water?

"All the fun's in how you say a thing."

'—Robert Frost

Most seasoned sales professionals probably will think that they can bypass this chapter because they have heard about features and benefits throughout their sales careers. And yet, many of the seasoned professionals who actively participate in features-and-benefits contests in my sales training seminars seldom exhibit a real understanding of this fundamental sales skill.

Let's see how *you* do on a simple features-and-benefits test. If you properly identify each item, you have an *excellent* grasp of the concept of features and benefits, and you should skip this chapter and move on to the more advanced chapters. If you are wrong on even *one* of the items, even though you may be just a little rusty, I urge you to read this chapter very carefully and commit the information contained in it to your memory bank.

FEATURES-AND-BENEFITS TEST

On a piece of paper, write down whether the following descriptions of a writing pen are features or benefits by placing an F (feature) or a B (benefit) beside the corresponding number.

1. Gold plated trim .00005″ thick
2. Spring clip will reduce likelihood of loss
3. 1½″-long spring
4. Weighs half an ounce
5. Imprinted with Gothic letters
6. Comes in a variety of designer colors
7. Constructed of aluminum
8. Hard point made out of titanium
9. Writes fine
10. Expensive
11. Slim design
12. Push-button retraction prevents ink leaks
13. Plastic cartridge holds one-tenth ounce of ink
14. Fine threads on barrel allow for tight connection
15. Black enamel
16. Lead-free enamel reduces health hazards
17. Cartridge
18. Comes with carrying case
19. Thirty-day warranty
20. Sold all over the world
21. Available in medium and heavy point
22. The pen of choice of industrial leaders
23. A matching pencil is available
24. Spring clip is made of spring steel
25. All-purpose eraser removes lead and ink
26. Ink eraser made of ninety-durometer rubber
27. Made in the United States

28. Manufactured by union labor
29. Ink will not run in 140°F temperature
30. Pen writes when held upside down

Answers

1. F	11. B	21. B
2. B	12. B	22. B
3. F	13. F	23. B
4. F	14. B	24. F
5. F	15. F	25. B
6. B	16. B	26. F
7. F	17. F	27. B
8. F	18. B	28. B
9. B	19. B	29. B
10. B	20. B	30. B

FEATURES AND BENEFITS DEFINED

What exactly are features and benefits? A feature describes the physical characteristics of a product or the specific aspects of a service. For example, the pen with which I am writing is constructed of aluminum and has a baked-enamel finish, and the manufacturer's name is imprinted on its side in five-point Gothic letters. It has gold trim that is .00005″ thick, a titanium fine ballpoint, a tempered-steel spring, a ninety-durometer rubber eraser, an interchangeable cartridge, black ink with nonrun pigment, and a spring-tension pocket clip. It costs $42. How many do you want?

If I were to describe the same pen using its benefits, I would describe it very differently. The pen is lightweight, has a durable finish, and is manufactured by a very well-known, reputable American company. Its gold trim is very attractive, a reflection of your good taste and style. The space-age ballpoint will enable you to write upside down and under water with consistently even distribution of the nonleak ink. The hardness of the eraser will last as long as the pen, and the interchangeable cartridge will enable you to use this exceptional pen for many years to come. You will be proud to show off this handsome writing instrument, and its sturdy pocket clip will enable you to wear it proudly while reducing the likelihood of loss or theft. This expensive-looking writing pen compares with similar pens selling for more than $100, yet it sells for less than $50. How many do you want?

DOES EVERYONE BUY BENEFITS?

If you sell technical products to Analytical buyers, sell features. Nothing will excite an Analytical physician or scientist more than lights, bells, and whistles. Because I used to think that *everyone* bought benefits only, I almost cost a salesperson a significant sale.

I was the National Sales Manager for a division of Honeywell, and David Davidinko was the Dallas area sales representative. We were selling biomedical engineering services to hospitals whereby we would repair medical equipment, service it on an emergency basis, and provide warranty service. We would replace out-of-tolerance electro/mechanical parts, uncover incipient malfunctions, and bring the equipment up to its original warranty condition.

David wanted to make a joint sales presentation. Prior to our meeting, we discussed the specific sales approach that we would use when meeting with the hospital medical director. David wanted to show some of our test fixtures and scientific standardization reports. I suggested to David that he should use his presentation time to address the increased patient safety and the reduction of hospital liability-insurance premiums associated with our programs. In short, I urged David to talk about the *benefits* of the program. I had been one of Honeywell's most successful salespeople in the entire country, so who would know better than I?

David, who was anxious to learn, accepted my suggestion, and we made our joint sales call. David introduced me to the physician and immediately began his presentation. After hearing David spend ten minutes describing the benefits of our services, I thought to myself that David had the $10,000-per-month order in the bag.

Using the direct close (which usually works very well with Analytical buyers), David asked for the order. "Well, Doctor, I believe that it is as apparent to you as it is to me that our program is an essential component of good health-care delivery. I need your approval now to begin service tomorrow." To my surprise, the doctor replied, "No, I believe we are better off doing business with the individual medical-equipment manufacturers. They have specialized test equipment and computer standardization forms. The manufacturer of centrifuges, for example, has a revolutions-per-minute gyro counter with a digital readout that is accurate within 1 percent. No, but thank you for your time. Mr. Whitlock, nice meeting you."

A sudden surge of stupidity overwhelmed me. I quickly asked the doctor to give us just a few more minutes, and I walked the doctor through every feature of Honeywell's program that I could recall. The doctor finally decided to buy our services.

Almost everyone buys products and services for the benefits, not for the features, *except* Analytical buyers. When you are buying a car and the salesperson opens the trunk, which sounds more exciting to you:

"Our deluxe model Panther has 13.4 cubic feet of trunk space," or

"Our deluxe model Panther has enough trunk space to accommodate the average family's storage-space requirements and then some. I know traveling salespeople who transport half their offices, samples, and clothes in this trunk at the same time."

If you are dealing with an Analytical or Situational personality, he or she will appreciate the 13.4 cubic feet sales pitch. If your prospect is a Persuasive, Assertive, or Friendly personality, he or she will generally relate better to the benefits of the trunk size.

EVERY FEATURE HAS A CORRESPONDING BENEFIT

Benefits tell the prospective buyer how the product or service will benefit its owner or user. Of course, if your competitor's product has more features than your product has, you always can counter with statements such as, "The more bells and whistles, the more that can go wrong." "The more frequently it breaks down, the more you won't be able to use it." Ask a Mercedes Benz salesperson why a Mercedes still is not equipped with power steering and he probably will tell you that power steering is an added repair burden or that it is not safe. Other good lines of defense against your competitor's product's features include:

- Their bell clangs too loudly and may injure one's hearing.
- If it were *truly* a necessary feature, *we* would have added it to our product.

These statements make it appear that your engineers had the knowledge and expertise about the feature, but in their infinite wisdom they decided that it would only drive the price up and hurt the consumer's pocketbook. Your competitor begins to look like a greedy, self-serving snake in the grass, while your company appears to be consumer oriented and price sensitive. Of course, *never* say anything bad about your competitor. But you certainly can point out the differences in your products and services.

There frequently is some confusion about features and benefits as they apply to the service industry. I once had dinner with Red Adair, the famous oil-fire consultant. If you were talking to his potential clients, how would you separate the features from the benefits of his fire-fighting services?

I'd have to say that Adair's technical expertise, equipment, insurance, and rates were his basic service features. His ability to go anywhere in the world on a moment's notice, his expert use of the most advanced equipment, and his ability to extinguish an oil-well fire at a competitive price in the shortest period of time were the benefits of his services.

If you are in a service business, ask yourself what assets are employed to deliver your service. Then ask yourself what specific benefits your customer gains from these assets. An insurance agent working for State Farm Insurance might consider that the size of her company is both an asset and a feature. The corresponding benefit, of course, is the comfort a customer would have knowing that when a catastrophe strikes, emergency money and services will be readily available. The huge variety of insurance options offered by the State Farm agent is a feature that other insurance salespeople may not have. The corresponding benefit is that the State Farm customer has only one agent to contact for automobile, health, home, and life insurance. As a sales professional with an agency such as State Farm, you should concentrate on benefits during your presentation unless your prospect has an Analytical personality. Even with the Analytical or Situational prospect, hedge your bet: For each feature you discuss, provide a corresponding benefit.

CAN YOU IDENTIFY THE BENEFITS OF YOUR
PRODUCT OR SERVICE?

No matter what you are selling, take a few hours and compile a comprehensive list of each feature of your product or service. Then identify at least one benefit for each feature on your list. In a seminar I conducted for IBM and *Entrepreneur* magazine, the attendees came up with more than 100 features and benefits of a Cross pen. Imagine what you can do with a computer, boat, refrigerator, attaché case, secretarial service, or bookkeeping service.

Take your time and thoroughly examine what you are selling. If it is a product, how is it constructed? Why is it designed the way it is? How does each feature help the consumer? You may uncover multiple benefits for just one feature. For example, a pen's ballpoint titanium tip enables the consumer to write evenly as well as upside down. If you are selling services, there generally are multiple benefits for each feature. For example, computerized reports connote increased accuracy, faster service, and more state-of-the-art accounting capabilities.

When you finish your features/benefits list on your product or service, do the same thing with your competitors' products or services. If you have difficulty doing this, some homework probably is in order. You should know your competitions' products or services as well as you know your own. By knowing your product or service and your competitors' products or services better than anyone else, you can enthusiastically convey the knowledge and professionalism essential to a successful sales career. In some arenas, the features list will be very important. If you are selling software programs to accounting firms or investment opportunities to financial planners, although you will want to commit to memory the significant features and benefits, you'll emphasize the features to your prospects. Even if your prospect does not have an Analytical personality, he or she will be concerned with the features. If, however, you are selling a nontechnical product or service, it's usually best to sell benefits.

If all everyone was interested in were features, any automobile with four tires, an engine, a steering wheel, a body, and an electrical system should meet those needs, and everybody would buy economy cars. People buy station wagons, however, because they meet family and business needs. People buy luxury cars because of ego and business needs, not to mention resale-value benefits. People buy sports cars, vans, two-door coupes, and four-door sedans for a variety of needs and benefits. You will make your sales by stressing benefits, so sell benefits.

WORK ASSIGNMENT

List ten features and ten benefits of each of the following products and services: a necktie, a secretarial service, your automobile, a cellular telephone, and your wristwatch. Then identify the features and benefits of the products or services you actually are selling.

8
The New Prospecting Formula

"Your ship will come in sooner if you're willing to swim out to meet it."

—Unknown

Prospecting plays a significant role in sales because without a solid prospect list, you'll be unable to build a lucrative sales territory. Finding prospects is one of the most critical phases of a salesperson's work. If a salesperson is not vigilant, he or she can be robbed of potential customers by aggressive competitors or by such routine events as retirement, relocation, death, bankruptcy, or simple turnover.

Sales prospecting is analogous to prospecting for precious metals. Just as a gold prospector looks for the mother lode using his pickax and the other supplies his old donkey carries, the sales prospector searches for qualified prospects using his sales tools. Unfortunately, sales prospecting is not so simple as loading a pickax and supplies onto a donkey and chopping away at the ground when you see interesting outcroppings. But sales prospecting can be as profitable as finding gold *if you know the best ways to prospect.*

DISCOVER MARKET NUGGETS

In every marketplace, there are market nuggets to uncover. If you are selling a rare antique automobile, there probably is a buyer who would buy it sight unseen if she only knew about it. Out of every 100 prospects, perhaps ten are qualified to buy, meaning that they have sufficient authority to buy and sufficient funds. Of those ten, perhaps two have an immediate need to buy. How do you find these two? Wouldn't it be nice if you could first sell to these qualified prospects who need your product and then sell the rest?

One of the best prospectors I know is an advertising saleswoman who works for a business newspaper in San Francisco. Each week, the editorial staff covers a specific market segment editorially. For example, the business editorial staff will write articles about the banks in the Bay Area the first week of the month. The second week, they will cover the business-products industry; the third week, they will write about the computer industry; and so on. Our enterprising sales professional contacts all the banks one to two months before the banks are covered editorially and sells the advantages of paid advertisements in the editorial section on banking.

In many respects, the newspaper does her prospecting for her because the editors decide what the editorial product will be, and she sells into that product. What bank would not want to advertise next to an article on the state of banking in San Francisco? Assuming that the state of banking is good, almost every bank in town is going to fight for an adjacent position!

Another soon-to-be-great prospector was selling printing services. He sold customized letterhead stationery, business cards, and brochures, and he offered his prospects good printing capabilities at competitive prices. He discovered very quickly that he had lots of competition, and many of his prospects had long-standing relationships that made it difficult for him to get his foot in the door.

Instead of giving up, he decided to target *new* businesses for they would need all the services that he had to offer. For his prospect list, he simply checked the new-business column in his local newspaper and called on the persons who had filed doing-business-as (dba) notices with the newspaper. He was the first salesperson on their doorsteps with a number of suggestions on how they could obtain quality products while keeping their printing costs down. Because all the prospects were just starting out, few had long-standing relationships with other printers. Every prospect was a strong potential customer.

This prospecting tool worked so well for the printer that he obtained new corporate filings from the state's Corporate Commissioner's office. He contacted the local chamber of commerce for a list of new members and called on all new businesses moving into the city. He contacted professionals, such as attorneys and physicians, as well as small business owners just moving into new offices and/or buildings.

Each and every prospect needed the printer's services. In the days of old, he found about four out of ten people who needed his services, and perhaps two of these were qualified prospects. Of the two, only one would be willing to try his services. Before he began prospecting through the new dba newspaper filings, the chamber of commerce's new membership directories, and new-construction magazines, he made ten calls a day, which produced one sale. With his newfound prospecting techniques, he located eight out of ten people who were qualified buyers, and he actually sold his printing services to six of the eight. Not only did he increase his sales 500 percent, but he began to establish long-term relationships that would mean repeat business, and he kept his competition's access limited for years to come.

Any stationery store, business-equipment company, attorney, or accountant could use the same sources as our printing salesman to develop a solid prospect list. Just mail each prospect a short letter with a special get-acquainted offer that's impossible to refuse.

REACH QUALIFIED PROSPECTS

Imagine landing in New York City where you do not have any business contacts. How many shoes, computers, or temporary-services contracts would you be able to sell? Very few, I would imagine. But where do you begin?

First, you must find people who need or want your product. Then, you must establish that the prospect has the ability to pay for your product. Third, you must make sure that the prospect has the authority to make the purchase. Does purchasing your product or service have any eligibility requirements? In other words, must your prospect meet specific qualification standards to purchase? Is the prospect accessible to you? The president of the United States may be a wonderful prospect for your secretarial services, but if you can't reach him to sell him on the idea, he's really not a viable prospect for you.

Can you identify your prospect? Perhaps your company already has a profile of buyers from its past research. If that's the case, you're halfway there. If you're making cold calls, you're basically relying on the law of averages to bring in qualified prospects. Cold calling can be a terrible waste of time, but it may pay off at times for certain types of door-to-door sellers. In most cases, part of the process of paying dues is the necessity to make cold calls as you're starting out. If you're forced to make cold calls, embrace the idea of building your territory personally and capitalize on your sales skills. Cold calls made in January can result in concrete sales in February. If you fail to generate leads in January, who will you sell to in February?

Ask existing customers for referrals. Don't eliminate friends, relatives, or acquaintances from your list, either; at the very least, they may be a source of referrals. Many very successful salespeople do not make cold calls anymore; they simply work on referrals. At some point in time, you, too, may rely almost totally on referrals. Your sales manager also may obtain leads for you from other departments in your company, such as from advertising (inquiries) or from the service department.

Rent Mailing Lists

How do you find your key prospects? Try renting mailing lists. Lists may be rented by zip code, income, age, street address, past product purchase history, household income, magazine subscriber lists—you name it. If you are selling oil-well tax shelters, for instance, rent the names of those who have invested in oil wells in the past from your local list broker instead of cold calling on unqualified prospects with little or no experience in oil prospecting. Each and every person you call on already should be familiar with depletion allowances, intangible drilling cost write-offs, and economic upside potential. Not only will your job be much easier, but your selling time will be well spent. The $60 to $120 per 1,000 names may be the best investment you ever made.

If you wanted to sell home refinancing, how would you find your prospects? You could go door-to-door and ask home owners if they would like to convert their equity to cash. You could buy advertising in your local newspaper or purchase radio or television spots if your advertising budget allows. You could send simple fliers or elaborate direct-mail pieces to home owners in your area. All these methods are used daily all over the country by people who want to sell home-refinancing services. At best, any of these methods will yield a mere 1 to 4 percent response on the average.

It's critical to consider how much each lead is costing you. If you are spending $500 a month for a billboard that only five people a month respond to, you are paying $100 a lead. This is pretty expensive prospecting. If just one out of the five who calls you actually buys, you are spending $500 for each new customer. If your product is a luxury car that sells for $100,000, the cost per lead may be acceptable. If you are selling $500 fax machines, you'd better find a more effective way to prospect for customers.

If I were selling home refinancing, I would rent lists of people who bought homes more than five years ago. With such a list, I would be assured that: 1) I am talking to the home owner; and 2) the home owner probably has accumulated equity.

To inquire about list rentals, look up "mailing lists" in the yellow pages.

Hire a Telemarketing Company

Next, I would check with several reputable telemarketing companies and request bids on handling an outbound (outgoing) telemarketing effort. After properly screening each firm, I'd select one telemarketing company to call the persons on my lists. The computerized telemarketing system dials the telephone number, and when someone answers, the telemarketing computer asks the party answering if he or she could use extra money during these difficult times. The listener hears how idle cash can be used for investment purposes, to put a child through college, or to consolidate other debts. If the prospect is interested, he or she receives instructions to ensure that the computer captures his or her name and telephone number.

Outbound telemarketing is an excellent way to obtain leads. If you elect to use an outside telemarketing firm, negotiate an agreement by which you pay for the leads generated instead of for the number of calls made. Using the telemarketers, determine as much as you can about each prospect's buying motives. Then, you should make a *personal* call on every lead generated by the telemarketing effort. Because the prospect has been prequalified, you should be closing 70 to 90 percent of those you call.

To put this in practical terms, if you were working on a commission and earned $50,000 the past year by selling one out of every ten prospects, you could earn seven to nine times that amount by prospecting correctly. Just imagine what your life would be like if your annual income skyrocketed from $50,000 to $450,000. When it is well thought out and properly focused, prospecting can be your ticket to tremendous sales success.

Investigate the reference section in your local library. You'll find lists of manufacturers, wholesalers, distributors, and importers and exporters of every imaginable product. The *Thomas Register* is a great source for prospecting industrial accounts. You also can locate association membership lists through your library. Most manufacturers' associations provide lists of manufacturers in each state that typically include the names of the owners, managers, and purchasing agents. Most major cities have hospital associations with membership directories that list the number of beds, the specialty health services available, and the names of department heads. Check with your local public library or university library before you buy or rent lists, books, directories, or membership rosters. What you need may be available for free.

THE QUESTION TO ASK

The essential keys to successful prospecting are first to identify who your qualified prospects are and then to ask yourself where you can find the greatest number of qualified prospects in the shortest period of time. Your answer should point you in the right direction for effective prospecting.

For instance, the person who needs denture cleaning solvent the most is someone who wears dentures. If you seek brand loyalty, give samples to dentists who, in turn, will give them to their patients who are denture cleaning solvent buyers. The fact that their dentists are giving them your samples is an implied endorsement. Why do you think pharmaceutical companies give millions of dollars worth of samples to physicians every year in the United States? Give the person in authority your product to dispense, and you should see your sales rise significantly.

Identify your prospect and reach him or her before your competition does. If you are selling diapers, senior citizens probably would not be your primary target group. Yet, a few grandparents may have grandchildren who spend a weekend from time to time, and there is an occasional change-of-life baby. But let's face it, you want new mothers who're about to leave the hospital. Give an initial supply of diapers to every new mother while she still is in the hospital. Don't give her the opportunity to go to the supermarket and select another brand. Establish brand loyalty in her mind by reaching her first.

In the following list of examples, I refer to numerous products and services and provide a corresponding list of prospecting suggestions. Even if I have not included your product or service, the basic concept will apply. Remember to ask yourself: Where can I find the greatest number of qualified prospects in the shortest period of time?

> *Secretarial service.* New business listings. New corporation filings. Hotels without in-house executive services. Seasonally affected businesses such as aviation, insurance, and travel.
>
> *Buick automobiles.* Lists of existing Buick owners. Former Buick customers who have not purchased a new automobile for three years. Lists of people with demographics comparable to the existing customer base.
>
> *Residential property in Miami.* Lists of people with annual incomes of $50,000 or more. Lists of individuals who've recently retired. Lists of human-resources managers who manage employee relocations for new employees.
>
> *Women's designer apparel.* Subscriber lists from women's publications with demographics similar to the demographics of your previous buyers. Lists of people who purchase women's apparel through mail-order catalogs. Lists of female managers and executives earning $40,000 or more per year.
>
> *Travel agency.* Airline frequent-flier lists. Cruise lines customer lists. Subscribers to travel magazines. Lists of small- to medium-sized companies.
>
> *Hammers.* Subscribers to craftsman magazines, do-it-yourself magazines, and tool catalogs. Lists of customers purchasing tools from catalogs. Membership rosters of carpenters' unions. Lists of buyers of home-remodeling books.
>
> *Wine.* Wine magazine subscriber lists. Wine club membership rosters. Wine connoisseur club membership lists. Lists of restaurant and bar owners.

> Lists of discount and retail alcoholic beverage buyers. Lists of visitors to wineries.
>
> *Yachts.* Lists of people with incomes of more than $150,000 per year by zip code (expensive and exclusive areas). Lists of owners of medium-sized boats. Graduates of Coast Guard–approved boating courses. Lists of members of yacht clubs.

If increasing your sales substantially is your goal, good prospecting techniques will help you achieve that goal. Prospecting should not be as hit or miss as finding a needle in a haystack or shooting an arrow at a target in pitch darkness. It is simply taking advantage of what is already available.

A former business associate of mine complained to me that his La-Z-Boy chair business had fallen off substantially. People simply were not buying his lounge chairs as they had in the past. He confided that his income had actually dropped from $85,000 the prior year to less than $40,000.

I wanted him to focus his attention on niche markets where product demand might be especially high. I asked him who needed his lounge chair more than anyone else? He thought for a moment before answering. "The handicapped and perhaps the senior-citizen market."

I agreed with him. I said, however, I thought most handicapped people sat in wheelchairs most of the time. At least most paraplegics and quadraplegics I know stay in wheelchairs, or shift themselves onto flat-bottomed, straight-backed chairs. Many handicapped people and senior citizens might have difficulty getting in and out of lounge chairs.

I asked him the same question again. "Who needs your lounge chair more than anyone else?" He shrugged his shoulders and answered, "Perhaps the middle-aged people who want to relax after a hard day's work." Yes, people of all ages would enjoy a comfortable lounge chair, most assuredly, including middle-aged people. For the third and final time I repeated, "Who needs your lounge chair the most?" A tad annoyed, he said, "People who stand on their feet all day, and newlyweds who have no furniture." Although senior citizens, retail salespeople who stand on their feet all day, and newlyweds in need of furniture certainly would appreciate the chairs and would be considered prospects, I told my friend that he continued to miss a very special niche opportunity.

There are thousands of hospitals with hemodialysis departments. There are tens of thousands of hemodialysis patients in the United States who must connect their veins and arteries to artificial kidney machines three to four times a week to clean their blood of impurities. To these people, these lounge chairs are near necessities. Each treatment can take as long as four to five hours. Hemodialysis patients *need* comfortable lounge chairs, and chances are pretty good that if a patient or a hospital buys a lounge chair, the chair will be tax deductible. For these people, the chairs can be written off as medical expenses. Consequently, they can own lounge chairs for considerably less than anyone else, and they may dialyze comfortably while reading or watching television in their own homes or in the hospital.

I urged my friend to buy the lists of individuals who subscribe to the dialysis newsletters and to invite the local subscribers into his store for a special lounge chair sale. He followed my advice and sales exceeded his greatest expectations.

Who needs your product more than anyone else? When you answer that question, you will know which group of people to pursue. Be as specific as possible. Then it is a simple matter of deciding which will be the most effective way to reach that select group. Whatever method you use, you will know that your chances for closing a sale have improved greatly for you've properly targeted your prospective customers.

KNOW YOUR AUDIENCE

This may appear self-evident, but always remember to sell first to that group of people who will give you the least resistance. Contact those who have a definite need for your products and services. You probably won't sell as many portable radios to people with hearing impairments as you will to beach-going teenagers who live in southern California. Nor will you probably sell as many calcium pills to young men as you will to middle-aged or older women who are more likely to be victims of osteoporosis, a problem primarily encountered by older women. You probably will sell more bubble gum to kids under fifteen than adults over forty. You probably will sell more airline tickets to traveling salespeople with regional or national territories and with incomes in excess of $100,000 than to teenagers under seventeen.

You must fully understand your audience and its needs to marry your product or service to the appropriate market. A well-planned, well-organized, targeted prospecting effort will save you countless hours of wasted sales time and increase your closing rate significantly. Evaluate your prospecting efforts regularly to ensure that you're getting a satisfactory number of the right kind of prospects cost effectively. Good prospecting is like investing money in a certificate of deposit. Closing a sale is removing the money, interest and all.

WORK ASSIGNMENT

The following list contains a number of products and services. In each case, ask yourself the key question: Who needs the product or service the most? Then write down the most promising consumer group you would target for each one.

Product or Service

Life insurance   Cellular telephone
Candy bar   Picnic basket
Computer paper   Snow skis
Mercedes Benz sedan   Watch
Golf clubs   Sod
Artificial Christmas tree   Lipstick
Office furniture   This book
Amateur telescope

9
Power Presentations That Work

*"A bore is a person who talks when you want
him to listen."*

—Ambrose Bierce

The most effective presentation is the one that gets the
order. If you can just walk in, show the product, get the
order, and be on your way to your next call in two minutes
flat, then keep up the good work! But, in my years of
experience, I'd have to admit that this probably is a pretty
rare occurrence.

PREPARATION

Preparation is absolutely essential! Woodrow Wilson was
once asked how long he took to prepare a ten-minute
speech. "Two weeks," he replied. He then was asked how
long it would take to prepare a speech lasting one hour.
"One week," he responded. When asked how much preparation was required for a speech lasting two hours, he
answered, "I'm ready now."

Your preparation and your attitude will be apparent to
your prospect almost immediately, so it is critical that you
are truly ready to give your prospect all you've got. The

better you know your subject matter and the more prepared you are, the more comfortable you will be during the
presentation and the more effective and exciting your presentation will ultimately be.

A prospect's needs and how you are going to help him or
her fulfill those needs always should be the basis of your
presentation. In *Presentations Plus* (Atlanta: John Wiley &
Sons), author David A. Peoples says that before a presentation you must first define your objectives by answering
the question, "Why are you making the presentation?" He
then recommends concentrating on the *close* of your presentation first because it's the most important part of the
presentation. Calling it the "bull's-eye," he suggests focus-
ing first on the center of the bull's-eye, then pulling back to
create the opening and body, always keeping your objectives in mind. If something doesn't work toward meeting
your objectives, don't use it. There's no sense dancing
around the issues and wasting your prospect's time. Speak
in specific terms and use relevant issues.

Peoples also objects to scheduling a question-and-an-
swer period at the end of a presentation because it detracts
from your closing. Instead, ask for questions *during* the
presentation so that when you're ready to close, all of the
prospect's questions will have been addressed and you can
ask for the order.

Get Organized

Obviously, you must organize your presentation materials
ahead of time. I'm a great believer in making a list of
anything I might possibly need, and gathering together all
the materials a few days before the actual meeting. Then I
double-check it all before I leave for the appointment. If
time is a luxury you don't have, prepare as much ahead of
time as humanly possible.

Check Out the Setting

If possible, familiarize yourself with the room where your presentation will take place and with any audiovisual equipment you'll be using. Determine the best seating arrangement, test the lighting and sound systems, check the acoustics, and note how the thermostat operates.

Carefully Select Your Clothing

How important is what you wear? It could be very important if you wear something inappropriate! The best advice is to wear something comfortable that you've worn before and know looks good on you. The impression you create is critical to relationship building and must be one of credibility.

The obvious advice is to dress conservatively in quality clothing, but there are going to be exceptions to that tried-and-true advice. Although people generally like it if you get dressed up for a special presentation, your choice of clothing depends on who you are calling on and your individual tastes. In certain industries, traditional business attire is a must, while in others a business suit would be totally inappropriate.

Don't let your style interfere with what you are trying to accomplish in your presentation. Unless your company has specific guidelines that you must follow, the best advice I can give you is to dress in a manner that suits your personal style and in a manner similar to your customer.

Practice Your Presentation and Time It

Rehearse until you feel so comfortable that you could throw away your script (which, by the way, is an excellent idea). Pay particular attention to your opening and closing so that you can begin and end your presentation smoothly, and with great confidence. Memorize the first three minutes because your opening is the most-listened-to segment of your presentation and sets the tone for the rest of your meeting.

Keep the presentation moving at a brisk pace and do not exceed the time limits you've been given. Think about what you are saying and how you are saying it. Anticipate any and all questions, and practice responding to each. Determine how potential problems will be handled *before* you give your presentation. Don't insult your prospect by trying to improvise.

Speak with Confidence and Authority

Keeping your voice strong will ensure credibility. As you practice, concentrate on one thought at a time, and speak in short, manageable groups of words. Using fewer words per breath helps ensure a concise, controlled flow of ideas.

Use your natural voice; don't force your voice for effect. Speak from your diaphragm instead of through your nose. To maintain audience interest and make an impact, vary the highs, lows, and volume of your voice. A little show of emotion is all right as long as your prospect doesn't think it is an act or merely part of a show.

Speak precisely but not too slowly. "Punch out" key words and emphasize any concepts that you want your audience to remember.

Match the Presentation to the Audience

Analyze your audience. Make sure that you know as much as you can about the individuals who will be in attendance. Who are the decision makers? What opinions are they likely to have already formed? What do they know about your company, your product or service, and you?

What questions or objections will they probably have? Are there any demographic characteristics that you should keep in mind? If you've done your homework, you should know not only who the players are but also their personalities and styles, and how best to interact with each.

Practice Positive Self-Imagery

The day before the presentation, clear your mind of all fears. First, imagine the absolute worst thing that could possibly happen, and determine how you would handle the problem. Then, know in your heart that you'll survive, even in the highly unlikely event that a disaster occurs.

Visualize yourself making the perfect presentation from start to finish. Psychologist Anees Sheikh, one of the country's leading experts on visualization, says that research has shown that mental practice can have the same effect as real practice. Likewise, Charles Garfield, researcher and author of *Peak Performers* (New York: William Morrow), reports that mental rehearsal provides a huge lift to the performances of individuals.

In your visualization, watch the customer reply positively to each of your points. See yourself getting the order and concluding the meeting on a successful note. Be specific in your visualization, and make it as real as possible to get the best results. Imagine everything from the moment you walk in the room to the moment you leave.

Build Rapport

Your immediate goal is to get the customer to take an active role in your presentation and make a commitment to your product or service. One essential point to remember: Identifying and solving your prospect's problem is your mission. It's always wise to find out before you begin if anything has changed since you last spoke. There may be some last-minute information that will have a bearing on what you say in your presentation.

Throughout your presentation you have the opportunity to fulfill your prospect's needs. To do this, you must build a relationship with everyone in the room.

To build rapport, you first must project an interested, helpful, positive attitude. Be upbeat and enthusiastic. Because you want to win the trust and confidence of those in attendance, the last thing you want to do is project an air of self-righteousness or arrogance. Open with a friendly greeting, and let your prospect know that you are grateful for the opportunity to speak with him or her. Try to make those present feel good about being there with you. And although this won't come as a surprise, good eye contact is mandatory for audience support and participation.

Relax and Enjoy Yourself

Don't take yourself too seriously, and don't overestimate the importance of your presentation in the scheme of things.

COMMUNICATION

In a study of major companies, the chief executive officers (CEOs) were asked what skill was most important to succeed in business. The long list included technical, analytical, and interpersonal skills. The CEOs were unanimous in their selection of communication skills as being most critical to business success. The chances of attaining the desired results—either personally or professionally—are slim at best when communication breaks down.

Understand the Needs of Your Listeners

Communication takes place for one of three purposes: to inform, to direct, or to request. Unclear communication will misinform and misdirect, and both the communicator and the listener will suffer. We often forget that verbal communication is a *two-way* flow of information that calls for both saying something and listening to something. After talking continuously for some time, Welsh poet Dylan Thomas reportedly remarked, "Somebody's boring me; I think it's me."

Why do people listen? Generally, people listen out of self-interest, because of the individual who is communicating, or because of how the individual is communicating. In a successful presentation, all of these factors are at work.

Author Kevin J. Murphy perfectly described the need to listen in *Effective Listening* (New York: Bantam Books): "We are each blessed with two ears and one mouth—a constant reminder that we should listen twice as much as we talk." If you are attempting to solve the prospect's problems and meet his or her needs, you must listen to the prospect. Being an effective listener means not only listening for content but also for context. So listen for total meaning.

If you show a lack of interest in someone's comments, you really are indicating to all present that you aren't interested in that *person*. Reflect the speaker's point of view when you respond. Remember: One of your tasks while giving a presentation is to make those present feel good about themselves. An important factor in making your presentation successful is being sincerely interested in your audience and in what they can contribute.

Be Aware of Nonverbal Communication

Communication can also take place even when no words are spoken. One *action* can express panic or fear more vividly than the spoken word. The tone of one's voice can convey emotions totally opposite of what is being spoken. What you don't say may be more important than what you do say. Be aware that what's going on inside of you may be readily determined by your audience through your physical stance, eye and facial movements, hand gestures, and other nonverbal expressions.

Yogi Berra perhaps said it best: "You can observe a lot just by watching." You, too, should be watching the nonverbal cues of those attending your meeting if you want to know how they are accepting you and the information that you are imparting to them. They may be resistant to what you are saying if the material is foreign to them, or they may feel threatened or intimidated if you're presenting a solution that they feel they should have uncovered. Are they nodding in agreement as you make each point? Be sensitive to audience reaction, look beyond the verbal responses to find the underlying meanings, and respond to nonverbal cues. If the audience is reacting unfavorably, you may need to change the way you are making your presentation.

Get the Prospect's Attention

Start with an attention-demanding statement. Begin with a statement or a question that goes right to the heart of the presentation. You might try a statistic that will alarm the audience, a rhetorical question, or a statement that would startle anyone hearing it.

One of the most effective presentation openers in the world is, "If I could prove to you that [my product will save you 50 percent on your water bill or that you'll look ten years younger], would you order my product today?" This initial approach accomplishes two things simultaneously: 1) It qualifies the prospect. Is he a decision maker? Does he have the resources to buy? 2) It places the burden of proof on you and presupposes the sale is made if you prove your point.

A very successful salesman in the home water-conservation business typically will ask a prospect, "If I can prove to your satisfaction that I can pay you 100 percent interest on your savings and you don't have to give me your principal money, would you buy my product?" Who would refuse to earn 100 percent on a portion of her savings if she had zero risks? Even with 7½ percent certificates of deposit at your local savings and loan, you are at risk. More than one savings and loan has gone bankrupt, and now there is serious talk about the Federal Deposit Insurance Corporation (FDIC) going broke.

The water conservationist then makes his proposition. "What I have is a chemical polymer that is placed about six inches under your lawn with a polymer planting machine. The polymer acts like an underground water faucet. When you water your lawn, the polymer accepts the water, much like filling a balloon with air. The polymer seeks an equilibrium with the dry ground around it. As the ground starts to dry up, the polymer releases its water to the dry ground. Your water bills may be reduced by as much as 50 to 60 percent.

"If you are paying $50 a month for water, you could save about $25 per month, or $300 per year. Because the polymer will last for five years, you will save $1,500, and more if the cost of water goes up. You might expect to pay $1,000 for such a great product installed in your lawn. If you order today, your cost is $90 for the polymer and $110 to have it installed in your 3,000-square-foot lawn. For a total cost of $200, you can have your entire lawn polymerized!

"Of course, the product is inert, completely safe, and degradable. Just imagine earning 50 percent on your money invested the first year and more than 150 percent each year thereafter. And because it is buried in your yard, your investment is perfectly safe! I would like to see a thief steal your polymer or a bank manager run off to Jamaica with it. You will have one of the greenest lawns in the neighborhood, make 50 percent on your money the first year, and 150 percent on your money every year for the next four years, *and* conserve our country's greatest resource—water. May we install the polymer next Wednesday or Friday?"

The customer has agreed to the order if you could prove your point, and you did. The question about whether or not to buy already has been resolved with this approach.

Begin with an attention-getting device. I often start my seminars holding a paper straw and a hard, uncooked potato. I ask a member of the audience to push the paper straw through the hard potato. The seminar attendee normally hands the bent straw and uncooked potato back to me expressing a sense of disbelief that the feat is possible. I take a paper straw and easily put it right through the potato. After a few seconds, I explain that there is only one way to put the paper straw through the hard, uncooked potato: You have to put your thumb over the end of the straw so that the air cannot escape. The straw acts like a solid-steel rod as long as the air is trapped inside. Once the straw is bent, it never will penetrate the uncooked potato. I use this relatively simple trick to illustrate how knowing just one single fact can make a significant difference in the outcome of a project.

Do you know any magic or sleight of hand that would catch your audience's attention? If not, find one of the many books available today that contains amazing facts and statistics that you could weave into your opening statement.

Talk to All of the Decision Makers at One Time

Do not be bashful. Ask your prospect to invite everyone who has anything to do with buying your product to your presentation so that everyone will hear the same story at the same time. Have you ever made a sales presentation to a prospect who promised to relay your information to the concerned parties in his or her office? Purchasing agents are especially notorious for not following through on this often-told promise, or worse yet, they forget what you actually said.

The smart door-to-door salesperson will attempt to get the product in front of a husband and wife at the same time. If you present your vacuum cleaner to one spouse and not the other, you lose control of the sale. You won't know what information will be added and what information will be deleted when your presentation is retold.

The wife asks you to hold the vacuum cleaner for her, subject only to her husband's approval. Essentially, the deal is completed because she says her husband never refuses her anything. All you have to do is pick up the check tomorrow night. Of course, when her husband comes home, he doesn't have the advantage of seeing your demonstration, witnessing your enthusiasm, or reading all of the product endorsement information. All he hears is that some strange person visited his poor, unsuspecting, gullible wife and convinced her to part with $600 for a vacuum cleaner. She just bought a vacuum cleaner last year from Sears for less than $300; why not buy two refrigerators or two lawn mowers?

Of course, the wife forgot to tell her husband that you offered to buy their old vacuum cleaner for $150. She forgot to mention that you offered a free two-year service agreement. The husband forgot that he now was paying Sears $43 a year for its service warranty agreement. You arrive the next day in anticipation of picking up his check and signed order only to be told "no" and to never darken their doorstep again. If you had made your presentation to the husband and wife *at the same time*, your potential sale might have become a real sale instead of a disappointment.

To better illustrate my point, the next time you are in a group of three or more people, use the technique that I use with my seminar attendees, which I discussed in Chapter 4. Ask one of them to silently read any paragraph from this book (or any reading material that's handy). After the first person has read the paragraph, ask him or her to whisper the content to the second person, who should whisper it to the third person, and so on. Then ask the last person to compare his or her understanding of the paragraph with what the first person read. Most likely the group will be shocked at just how distorted the information has become.

People usually do not distort information intentionally. They simply fill in any blanks with additional information to complete an idea in their own minds. If at all possible, make your presentations to all the decision makers at once. Do not allow distortion to cost you your sales commission. Deal with any objections the prospect has and close the sale on the spot.

AUDIOVISUAL AIDS

Audiovisual aids can be tremendously beneficial to a presentation if they are used appropriately. University studies have revealed that people are much more likely to be persuaded if visual aids are used. These aids help emphasize key concepts, illustrate important points, lend support, and clarify information not readily understood or fully appreciated when presented just orally. But beware. Audiovisuals can *detract* from your presentation by overpowering you, or they may distract the audience from your message if they are not properly coordinated. Any audiovisual aid requiring too much explanation probably is defeating its purpose. You should match the audiovisual aid to the specific requirements of the presentation.

The one audiovisual aid that has more impact than all of the other audiovisual aids is, of course, your product. If possible, always show the product instead of a video, slide, transparency, or photograph of it. Other audiovisual aids appeal only to the prospect's sense of sight and hearing. The actual product brings *all* of the prospect's senses into play.

One essential point to remember: Audiovisual aids *never* should be a substitute for a walking, talking, breathing, thinking salesperson! Employ them only as additions to your presentation; they never should be the entire presentation.

To minimize the potential problems of your audiovisual presentation, use your own equipment if possible. Be prepared for mechanical problems. Make sure you have any necessary spare bulbs and an extension cord on hand, and know how to operate all of the equipment. Have a contingency plan ready in the event that you are unable to use the audiovisual equipment or if it malfunctions halfway through your meeting. If you are traveling by plane or train to your presentation, always carry your materials with you instead of stowing them in the baggage compartment. Unfortunately, I know firsthand that bags get lost.

Following is a list, in order of greatest impact on the customer, of audiovisual aids that are available to you:

Product itself
Videotape
Slide presentation
Overhead transparencies
Desktop presentation book

Videotape

Although there are exceptions to every rule, in general, never use photographs, overheads, or slides in a demonstration if you have a professionally produced, current video. A good video presentation tells a consistent sales message in a professional manner.

A good video will spur the viewer to action. A video presentation usually should last between three to six minutes. It could have a strong introduction with music and images of your home office, employees working diligently, and manufacturing equipment producing your product. Images of quality control, personnel checking production output, and trucks loaded with your products pulling away from your dock always are impressive. Brief interviews with management and regulatory agencies work extraordinarily well, and success stories from satisfied customers command attention.

A good video works. It guarantees that every customer who views it will be exposed to every salient point you want to make sure he or she hears. Customers seldom take telephone calls or allow interruptions during a video presentation, which results in a consistently high level of commitment. A video allows you to show your plant, equipment, management, employees, customers, corporate culture, or any other information that you simply could not present unless your prospect was willing to personally visit your plant and interview your management and customers (which a prospect normally is not willing or able to do).

A good three- to six-minute video will cost between $3,000 and $25,000 depending on what you want the final product to contain, whether a mobile crew is required, whether one or two cameras will be used, how much editing is required, and the experience of your producer. Of course, you probably won't require a lot of expensive special effects, but if you do, expect the costs to soar.

The operative words when ordering video production services are past performance and price. A video company should show you five to ten high-quality videos they've produced and provide you with references that you should check out. Make certain that the company will produce storyboards (which tell the director how each scene should be shot) along with a script. Attend each shoot and sign off after each scene is recorded so that there will be few surprises for you later. Of course, much can be lost in the editing process, so if possible, attend the editing sessions.

If you can demonstrate significant earnings over the past few years, you may be able to persuade a video production company to enter into a partnership arrangement with you. I know one bright computer salesperson who called on industrial accounts. She convinced a video production company to produce a video in exchange for her agreement to sell their services to her client base. She put the 10 percent commissions toward the $7,200 cost of producing her videotape. Within three months, she had sold $72,000 worth of video production services, and her debt was paid off. She did so well that she now sells video production services full-time.

A video is an almost essential sales tool, so if your company doesn't have a professionally produced video, talk to your employer about having one produced. If your request falls on deaf ears, perhaps your employer would consider splitting the cost with you, or maybe you should consider producing one by yourself. The potential for increased sales should justify the expenditure. One multilevel marketing sales professional increased his earnings from $14,000 a month to more than $400,000 a month when he began selling three-minute videos to each prospective customer. One of the best video production companies I know of is The International Television Production Company located at 448 East 6400 South, Suite 210, Murray, UT 84107, (800) 231-0048.

Videocassette recorder (VCR) equipment is easy to use. All-in-one color televisions and VHS portable videotape players are available by Emerson for $800 to $900. Radio Shack sells a nine-inch portable VCR for less than $700. Videotapes can be readily duplicated, erased, and reused, as well as conveniently stored or mailed.

Slide Presentation

A professional slide presentation can make a great impression. You can easily carry a slide projector and carousels on your sales calls. With several interchangeable carousels, you can have one carousel preloaded with a presentation for one customer and a second preloaded for another. If you were selling oil wells to end-users and wholesalers, you could tailor each presentation to a specific audience by having two (or more) sets of preloaded slides.

One major advantage with slides is that you can make your own slides with a good 35mm camera. You can buy slide film from most camera stores and department stores that have photography sections. Another significant advantage of slides is that you can change portions of your presentation without having to redo the entire audiovisual aid (as you would with a video).

Slide advance can be manual, or it can be keyed to an audible signal added to the tape so that, as your customer listens to an audio presentation that you've taped, the machine flashes the slides automatically. I am not completely sold on this system, however, because it doesn't allow you to interject comments, concentrate on slides of specific interest to your customer, or alter your presentation to fit the immediate sales situation.

A slide projector with audiocassette programming and front- and rear-screen projection by Telex will cost about $1,000, while projectors with fewer bells and whistles will run anywhere from $600 to $900. Remote controls, bulbs, and extra slide trays are additional costs.

During your three- to six-minute slide presentation, introduce your prospect pictorially to your product, plants, or manufacturing operations. Show your prospect graphs or charts that visually reflect high customer satisfaction and favorable competitive comparisons. If your prospect has any particular concerns, take a little extra time on the one slide (or slides) that addresses his or her concerns before moving on with your presentation.

Match the proper audiovisual aid to the presentation. If you are selling pencils to retail stationery stores, a slide presentation probably is not necessary. If, on the other hand, you are selling a charity to industrial benefactors, a slide show illustrating all the good works your organization accomplishes is most appropriate.

A well-organized, properly targeted collection of slides can keep your presentation on track and on schedule. It can hold your prospect's undivided attention and enable you to visually bring important supporting information into focus (forgive the pun!). Don't forget: It's best not to darken the room completely, or you may lose your audience to a five-minute nap.

Overhead Transparencies

An overhead presentation is an inexpensive but quite effective way to deliver information. An important testimonial letter can be copied onto a transparency for little more than the cost of a photocopy. Do you have copies of your new ad campaign, equipment specifications, competitive analyses, or informative graphs or charts? If so, put them on transparencies. It is one thing to tell a prospect that the Federal Bureau of Investigation (FBI) is buying your lie detector equipment; it is quite another to display a copy of the purchase order—magnified ten to twenty times.

An overhead transparency should not be used merely to repeat the text of what you're saying; instead, it should list, summarize, support, or enhance your comments. Use color and cartoons or other graphics to enliven your overheads.

Call your prospect's office several days ahead of your scheduled appointment and ask him or her to arrange for an overhead projector for your presentation. If one's not available, bring one of your company's or your own personal projector, or rent one from an office-supply store, camera store, or audiovisual equipment outlet.

A wide array of standard overhead projectors and portable models are available from manufacturers such as Polaroid, Elmo, Apollo, and 3M for from $400 to $1,200. Polaroid offers an instant transparency film system that includes a ProPack camera and special film that allows you to make small-format, color overhead transparencies of what you photograph in just a few minutes. A zoom projector is required for proper viewing.

You can set an overhead projector on most tables and project your transparencies on a screen, or even most walls, if necessary. As you place a transparency on the projector, you can address each topic as your audience reviews the information with you. On transparencies listing important items, you might want to reveal each point as you discuss it rather than "showing your hand" all at once and having the audience read ahead of you. This can be done using sequential transparencies with points that build on each other, or by physically covering with a sheet of paper all but those points being discussed.

Because you can write on a blank transparency with a

dry marker that wipes off clean, you can spontaneously illustrate a cost analysis or clarify a certain point in front of the entire group.

As with a slide presentation, when showing overhead transparencies, refrain from turning off all the lights. Mounting frames are useful because they make handling easier, and the frame covers the harshly lit edges of the screen. Writing numbers on the frames eliminates the possibility of out-of-sequence viewing.

Desktop Presentation Book

Self-standing desktop "flip chart" books usually contain ten to thirty plastic pockets in which to put your sales materials and are generally available in stationery or office-supply stores.

I usually design my desktop presentation to coincide with the chronological flow of my sales presentation. If I were selling office file cabinets, the charts in my presentation book might appear as follows:

1. Name of company in bold type
2. Chart of my company's advantages
3. Photo of product
4. List of product features and benefits
5. Copy of magazine advertisement(s)
6. Copy of customer testimonial(s)
7. List of satisfied customers
8. Competitive price comparison
9. Warranty
10. Order form

In less than five minutes, I can point out that my company is substantial and should be taken seriously. My product is aesthetically pleasing, competitive, and well advertised. Customers are satisfied with it, and it carries a significant warranty. Using my desktop book, no matter how often I give my presentation, I consistently include the same information in an organized manner because each page triggers a corresponding explanation. Yet, I still can tailor my presentation to the individual.

Similar to the desktop version is the larger flip chart typically perched on an easel. Although easy to make, easy to revise, and economical, this chart is not long-lasting, is very informal, and can be awkward to carry. It can, however, be extraordinarily effective in the appropriate setting if the presenter can talk, write, and draw all at the same time.

Handouts

If you wish to distribute printed information to those present, time your distribution properly so it does not detract from your presentation. You should control the audience's attention, so unless the handouts will enhance the specific points you are making at the time, don't pass them out until the end of your presentation. When handout materials are being distributed or read silently during a presentation, don't try to continue speaking until you regain everyone's full attention.

FOLLOWING THE PRESENTATION

Always take some time after the presentation to review what happened. This is your opportunity to identify not only what went wrong but also what *worked*. Analyze each part of your presentation from its opening to its close. Consider everything from the physical setting to the psychological impact of what you said. If possible, get feedback from your prospect.

Did you communicate well? Did you really listen to what those attending said? Were your audiovisuals appropriate? What would you do differently next time under the same circumstances? Consistently completing such an analysis following each presentation should help you produce more effective presentations in the future, which should mean more sales and more money in your pocket!

WORK ASSIGNMENT

It's easy to *think* you are communicating effectively, but how are you *really* doing? On a separate piece of paper, number from one to twenty-three. Consider each of the following twenty-three statements and write "Always," "Some of the time," or "Don't think about it" by each number.

1. I recognize that communication is hard work.
2. I know what must be said before I speak or write.
3. I identify which method of communication (in person, over the telephone, in writing) is best to have my message fully understood.
4. I think about my audience—who they are, what their level of interest is likely to be, and what their level of understanding is.
5. I identify my prospect's problems and offer solutions to those problems.
6. Prior to every presentation, I practice positive self-imagery to clear my mind of fears.
7. I am prepared when I make presentations.
8. I choose the right words for the subject and the audience and avoid the use of slang and jargon if it's inappropriate.
9. I select the audiovisuals most appropriate for each occasion.

10. I begin each presentation with a statement of purpose that is attention getting.
11. I speak with confidence and authority.
12. I let each customer know how much I appreciate the opportunity to meet with him or her.
13. I try to be interesting.
14. I am aware of the physical environment and its impact whenever I communicate.
15. I look for feedback from customers and business associates.
16. I listen with the same level of interest that I want given to me.
17. I listen for both context and content.
18. I seek a common understanding when communicating.
19. I am patient and listen when others are speaking, even if they are communicating ideas that are contrary to my own.
20. When communicating, I keep my points pertinent to the task at hand.
21. I am aware of nonverbal clues from my prospects and customers.
22. I am conscious of the impression that I make on others.
23. I maintain good eye contact with individuals, whether in one-on-one encounters or in meetings, or when making a presentation to more than one person.

To determine your score, give each statement a score based on the corresponding values assigned below:

"Always" = 1 point

"Some of the time" = 2 points

"Don't think about it" = 3 points

If your total score is 28 or less, you are a superb communicator. Go to the head of the class.

If your score is between 29 and 44, you probably are an effective communicator some of the time, but when communicating, you should consider those items that you rated a 2 or 3 more often than you currently are doing. You must focus on those specific areas where you are weakest to be an effective communicator on a more consistent basis.

If you scored 45 or more, you probably frequently misdirect or misinform when you communicate. When requesting one thing, do you often get another? You must become serious about improving your communication skills. Find books, audiotapes, and videotapes specializing in listening and speaking techniques; take notes and practice what you've learned. Have friends and associates that you respect critique your presentation style, including your body language and other unspoken communication modes.

10
Probing Made Easy

"Judge a man by his questions rather than by his answers."

—Voltaire

Probing means exploring and investigating. One of the simplest ways to probe is to ask questions. If you do not ask questions, you never will know whether or not your prospect has the resources or the authority to buy what you are selling. You won't have a clue about when your product or service will be needed or how much is required. You won't know the prospect's past purchasing history, pricing history, competitive tie-ins, or financing needs, or who the other influential decision makers are. There are myriad factors that you should know before you can do an effective selling job.

A ROAD MAP

The first questions a Realtor should ask you when you inquire about purchasing a house are:

- In what price range are you looking?
- In what area do you want to live?

- What kind of home are you looking for?
- How much of a down payment can you afford?
- Is the purchase of your new home contingent on the sale of your existing home?

The answers to these questions serve as a road map for the professional real estate salesperson.

In What Price Range Are You Looking?

The answer reveals what size mortgage the prospect can manage on a month-to-month basis and allows the Realtor to eliminate specific neighborhoods and specific homes to focus on what's affordable.

In What Area Do You Want to Live?

The area desired by a buyer may not necessarily be an *affordable* area. A buyer who qualifies for a $150,000 home may be able to get a four-bedroom, two-bath home in an average community, or a two-bedroom, one-bath house in a more exclusive area. A knowledgeable Realtor will explain the going rates for homes in the desired area and present alternatives to the buyer. If the buyer has a modest income and six children and can afford a small down payment, he may need to look at property outside the city where property values may be considerably less.

What Kind of Home Are You Looking for?

The answer to this inevitably leads to additional questions. How many bedrooms are needed? Is a formal dining room necessary? Is a two-car garage a must? Is your style of living more formal or informal? Do you like Tudor, colonial, or ranch-style homes? A split-level, one-story, or two-story house? Large or small yard?

How Much of a Down Payment Can You Afford?

What kind of financing does the prospect need? A real estate sales pro probably will continue with credit questions after this question is asked. If the prospect has less than good credit, the agent may discuss Federal Housing Administration (FHA) takeover possibilities; in these cases, the buyer's credit normally is not an issue because the seller often remains "on the hook" for several years after the sale. If the prospect offers a significant down payment (25 percent of the sale price), some lenders may guarantee a loan regardless of the buyer's credit history. The theory is that if a home owner has that much money invested and foreclosure occurs, in most cases the lender will have enough excess equity available to recover the entire loan after sales commissions are paid.

Is the Purchase of Your New Home Contingent on the Sale of Your Existing Home?

The answer to this question discloses whether or not the buyer can buy immediately. It also will indicate how much equity might be transferred to the new home purchase. Even if the prospect's income is modest, he or she may have significant equity in an existing home that would make the monthly payments for a new home very affordable.

Probing for such information enables the real estate sales professional to provide the prospect with a total, comprehensive service. She can analyze the customer's geographical and financial requirements along with his physical, psychological, and social needs and desires to meet the customer's ultimate goal: finding the ideal home in the shortest period of time, at the lowest possible price, with the best possible financing. The sooner the real estate sales professional accomplishes this incredible feat, the sooner the sale will be made. If you probe intelligently, your sales successes will grow exponentially.

BRAIN SURGERY OR ASPIRIN?

Imagine going to your family physician with the complaint that you have a migraine headache. You exhibit no other symptoms except that your head hurts. Unless the physician asks you a series of pertinent questions, he can only guess about the source of your problem. His diagnosis depends in large part on his probing skills. If he is wrong in his diagnosis, you could end up having brain surgery when all you needed was a prescription for a painkiller (or vice versa).

A good family physician is one of the best probers in the world. He may ask you when the headaches started and how frequently you have them. He will want to know if you wear glasses and when you had your last eye examination. Is your migraine headache accompanied by blurred vision, crossed eyes, or floating black dots in your vision? Are you experiencing a great deal of stress? He will inquire about your family medical history, take your blood pressure, and determine other vital signs. All of this information will help him establish a basis for diagnosis. Based on his diagnosis, he will recommend a solution. It may be a prescription, further tests to better pinpoint specific possibilities, or simply a recommendation to stop working so hard.

BE A COUNSELOR

Through probing, a sales professional may become a counselor. Even though your prospect may not be aware that she has a problem, she needs someone who can provide solutions. As a knowledgeable person, you are able to offer guidance and advice. As a salesperson, your task is to find out what problems your prospect has, acknowledge the existence of the problems, and then offer solutions. (For more information on this topic, refer to Chapter 14, "The Most Miraculous Selling Strategy.")

If it had not been for "solution" selling, my most successful sales experience would have been a sales disaster! I was selling biomedical engineering services, and month after month, I'd call on hospital engineers, administrators, and staff physicians, in an attempt to sell them a comprehensive equipment-maintenance service program. For a fixed monthly fee, my employer would bring a dozen factory-trained representatives into the hospital and bring each piece of medical, laboratory, and surgical equipment up to its original warranty condition. My technicians would uncover all incipient malfunctions and replace any out-of-tolerance components. Because of my services, hospital staff working with life-support respirators or any other medical device would not have so much cause to worry about malfunctions.

Every hospital employee who listened to my short presentation loved the concept, but *nobody* bought my program. I heard objection after objection. "It is too expensive." "No one company can service everything effectively." "It ain't broke, so why fix it?" "*I* want your service, but I can't get the rest of the staff to agree to buy it."

Of course, every hospital administrator asked the same painful, heart-wrenching, most-difficult-to-answer question: "Who else in the area is using your service?" I reasoned that if I could get just one prestigious hospital to buy, the rest surely would follow. But I couldn't even refer to satisfied hospital customers *anywhere else in the United States!* Although the other forty-two biomedical engineering salespersons were in the same boat I was, mine was sinking fast.

Imagine a whole year going by with not one sale. I had to either sell a hospital on our program, get another job, or go hungry. Unfortunately, no one was going to hire a salesman who had sold nothing for an entire year, and hunger seemed just too painful, so I took drastic measures. A year later, I had more than eighty hospitals as customers, my little southern California office was billing more than $5 million a year in service fees, and I was earning a 10 percent commission. Happy days were here again, and I had probing to thank.

What did I do? I launched a free hospital-evaluation survey program. I asked the hospital's chief engineer if he would allow me to survey his staff, evaluate his medical equipment, and give him a thorough report listing estimated downtime, inoperable equipment, and electrical safety recommendations—all free of charge. I then asked for a letter from him introducing me to the department heads so that they would give me access to their equipment. Each hospital engineer I approached agreed.

As I moved from department to department and presented the chief engineer's letter, the department heads opened up. One emergency room nurse told me about a young female victim of an auto accident who had suffered cardiac arrest and needed an external chest resuscitator (automatic cardiopulmonary resuscitation or CPR). The child recovered beautifully. Unfortunately, when a forty-six-year-old obese male was brought into the emergency room suffering from a heart attack, a solenoid malfunctioned, driving the plunger right through his chest. The surgery nurses told me about patients being electrocuted because grounding plates were not connected. Dialysis patients had died of air embolisms because the hospital did not have the air-bubble detectors repaired.

The list of deaths caused by malfunctioning equipment grew. One patient was electrocuted in the coronary-care unit after a nurse who was wearing nylon underwear walked across a nylon-carpeted floor in a nonhumidity-controlled room and touched a patient, accidentally discharging 300,000 volts of static electricity into the patient's external pacemaker. On completion of my investigation, I called to make an appointment with the Director of Administration.

At first, the administrator's secretary gave me a hard time about seeing him. When I explained that the hospital was going to lose its accreditation if the director did not meet with me, however, she readily set up an appointment. I was outraged that no one had done anything to correct the problems that had caused these horrible accidents. The air-bubble monitors still were waiting to be repaired, the external resuscitator still was 800 miles away being repaired, and the nurse still was wearing nylon underwear (I presumed).

"You Are Killing People!"

On arrival at the administrator's office, I showed him my survey results. I exclaimed, "Before I conducted my survey, neither one of us knew the extent of the hospital's equipment problems. I'm sure that if you knew what was going on, you would have done something about it. Now that we both know, something indeed has to be done. If a wrongful-death action were to be brought against the hospital, you possibly could be charged with criminal negligence. The press would have a field day with the unnecessary fatalities that have resulted because your hospital doesn't have an adequate preventive maintenance program."

After showing my prospect that he had a problem that needed solving, I then offered him my solution: a complete proposal for a comprehensive biomedical engineering program. He readily signed the agreement and I had my first hospital under contract! The survey program worked over and over again. Not all of the hospitals had as many problems as my first hospital, but I had an ever-increasing list of satisfied customers as a reference base.

Success breeds success. Thomas Jefferson once stated, "I'm a great believer in luck, and I find the harder I work the more I have of it." I'd like to replace *harder* with *smarter*.

My employer wanted me to fly back to Maryland and share with the other forty-two salespeople the almost-magical way in which I had suddenly sold so many hospitals in such a short period of time. Unlike a magician, who will not disclose how he performs a sleight of hand, I will reveal the mechanics of the "trick" to you: The secret, ladies and gentlemen, was probing.

ASK THE RIGHT QUESTIONS

You cannot sell solutions if you don't know what the problems are. Although I called it a survey, it was simply a way to probe effectively. My probing technique resulted in an income of more than $500,000 for me that year.

Instead of dominating the conversation with a prospective customer, a salesperson using the Socratic method (which has been around since 400 B.C.) systematically asks questions and actively listens to the answers to determine a customer's needs. You are on a fact-finding mission, but by probing, you also help your prospect understand his or her needs. A question-based meeting allows prospects to develop their own reasons why your product or service is what they need. Involving the prospect through probing helps break down any resistance he or she may have to changing to your product, and it helps build a relationship between the two of you.

Of course, you must ask the *right* questions, given your product or service and the individual prospect. You must learn what questions will work for *you* with each customer and potential customer. Many a medical misdiagnosis is the result of a physician not asking the right questions. *How* you ask questions also may determine the outcome of your probing effort. Ask questions sincerely and with interest. Show your concern for your prospect's problems. Let your prospect know that you understand his or her needs and are committed to finding a solution to his or her problems.

When developing the list of questions that you want to ask a prospect in a fact-gathering meeting, consider the kind of information you are after. A closed-ended question asks for a simple, direct answer, while an open-ended question asks for an explanation. If you want an in-depth, lengthy explanation and additional information volunteered by the prospect, an open-ended question works best. Closed-ended questions usually are more time efficient for they result in shorter responses, but the prospect may feel as if he or she is being interrogated. To encourage prospect participation, it's usually best to employ more open-ended questions, but toss in a closed-ended question on a regular basis for a change of pace and to maintain conversational control.

No matter what you are selling, initially you need some basic information from your prospect. For instance, if you are selling a diaper service, you certainly want to make sure your prospect has a baby. If you are selling consulting services, you will want to know if the prospect has ever used a consulting service, or if he or she is using a consulting service now.

Begin by asking your prospective customer if it is all right if you ask a few questions to get a better understanding of his or her business. Ask if you may take notes, and then write down his or her answers as well as any items you need to follow up on. Interview your prospects; don't grill them. Be genuinely interested in their responses. Smile and assure your prospects that their answers will be kept confidential and will enable you to better service their needs. Do *not* try to win over your prospects by sharing information about their competitors. If you are talking to your prospect about his or her competitors, then your prospect may reasonably conclude that you are talking to competitors *about him or her.*

The three basic categories of questions are general, competitive, and product specific. You must probe in all three areas to get the information required to provide solutions and to be of maximum value to your customers.

General questions would include anything that you ask about your customer's business and way of doing business, such as:

- How long has your company been in business?
- Have you filled out a credit application?
- Who is the decision maker?
- Have you bought from us in the past?
- Do you pay net thirty days?
- Do you have other divisions?
- Is your company public or private?

Competitive questions would include anything that you ask about your competitors and your competitive position. Examples would be:

- Who are you buying this product from now?
- How much are you paying now?

- Does my competitor ship FOB his plant or your plant?
- What kind of support is my competitor giving you?
- Do you have a long-term contract with my competitor?

Product-specific questions include anything that you ask about your customer's specific product requirements, such as:

- Do you want it in red or blue?
- How many do you need?
- When do you need it?
- Would you like to lease or buy?
- Do you require training?
- What sizes do you want?

Finally, ask your prospect to daydream for a moment and ask him or her what would be the *ideal* solution to his or her buying need or problem. This accomplishes two important things:

1. It makes your prospect consider why he or she should change his or her current supplier.
2. The prospect sells himself or herself on the idea that there might be a better way to meet his or her needs.

Your job is to show the prospect how your product can provide what he or she is missing. If for some reason the prospect can't immediately think of any improvements he or she would like to see, make suggestions that highlight the strengths of your company and its product.

Although you can continue to probe throughout the presentation, try to find out as much as you can *before* you start. Armed with the right answers, you can tailor your presentation to meet the needs of your prospect. If, for example, the prospect knows your company has a great reputation, don't waste a lot of presentation time on your company's strengths. If he or she is not the decision maker, find out who is, and invite that person to sit in on your presentation.

SELL SOLUTIONS

If you probe effectively, you can "solution sell." The solution salesperson is one of the strongest closers in most organizations. Pareto's Law states that 20 percent of your customers generate 80 percent of your sales. I believe that 20 percent of every sales force does 80 percent of the company's business, and I have found that 80 percent of most companies' sales come from *solution salespeople.* People will buy solutions to their problems, so present ideas to fill their needs. If you want to rise to the top of any sales force, your job is to probe effectively, to find out what your prospects' problems are, and then sell them solutions to those problems.

WORK ASSIGNMENT

It's time to test your skills in probing the customer effectively. On a piece of paper, list ten questions you would ask a customer in each of the following scenarios.

1. I want the Mercedes two-door convertible. My wife wants the four-door sedan.
2. We have been using Modern Office Supply Company for as long as I have worked here. I doubt if we would change vendors under any circumstances.
3. Consultants charge too much and do too little in my opinion.
4. We cannot afford your copy machine. Quite frankly, I wish we could.

5. Our customers prefer cotton instead of synthetic fibers.
6. Pens? Do I buy pens? I do not buy from the manufacturer; I buy only through wholesalers because they
   carry hundreds of product lines. If I tried to buy from
   each manufacturer directly, I would *never* go home!
7. You folks need to sharpen your pencil a little more.
   Your prices are always too high.
8. I will buy everything that you can ship in the next two
   days. We need electronic parts really badly. I know you
   are out of stock. What can you do for me?

11
Surefire Ways to Turn Objections into Sales

"Obstacles are those frightful things you see when you take your eyes off your goals."

—Unknown

The American Heritage Dictionary defines an objection as "a statement presented in opposition. A ground, reason, or cause for expressing opposition."

Although I cannot argue with that definition in general terms, in sales terms I view an objection differently; *an objection is simply a request for more information.* If you've qualified your prospect and that prospect has all of the correct information, he or she should not have an objection. If he or she does object, you should welcome the objection as just one more invitation to sell your product or service.

Let's assume that you are selling temporary secretarial services. You charge $20 an hour for a highly competent secretary who types 120 words per minute and is proficient in both WordPerfect and Lotus 1-2-3. Your competitors are charging comparable rates.

After making your presentation, your prospect tells you

that she can hire a regular, full-time secretary with identical skills for less than what you're charging for temporary services. She thanks you for stopping by and asks you to keep in touch.

Clearly, the prospect does not understand the benefit of using a temporary service. Temporary secretarial personnel can be brought into a business during peak periods to handle increased work loads, and they can be terminated as the volume drops off. This service gives management control over its costs while allowing work to proceed normally without interruption.

If an employer were to include all of the employee benefits a full-time employee receives in addition to his or her salary, she would find that using a temporary secretarial service actually may be cheaper than hiring a regular, full-time employee, only to lay off that employee as the work load wanes. Many of these cost factors are normally hidden or ignored, so you would want to walk the prospect through the process and reveal the real costs associated with a full-time employee.

Your prospect proposes to hire a new secretary for $18 an hour. But what does this person *really* cost the company on an hourly basis?

When you add in all of the company benefits (including paid time off for vacation, personal time, sick time, bereavement leave, and jury duty), the additional cost a company incurs per employee usually is anywhere from 30 to 40 percent of his or her salary. Using an average benefits cost of 35 percent, that means that an $18 an hour employee really is receiving an hourly rate equivalent to $24.30 per hour! Your quote for a temporary-services secretary is $20, and your firm is responsible for everything.

Did I mention that with regular employees an employer also has to be concerned with wrongful-termination lawsuits, unfair-labor-practice investigations, unemployment-compensation claims, workers-compensation claims, employee-relations problems, and countless employee-rights claims that fill our judicial systems dockets from one end of our country to the other? If your prospect knew all of the laws and potential liability associated with full-time employees, you probably could convince her not to ever hire another employee directly!

The salesperson should respond to her prospect's pricing objections by acknowledging the prospect's concerns. "Thank you for bringing that up. Here is a cost analysis for you to review." (See the sample chart that follows.) Ob-

SAMPLE COST ANALYSIS

Cost to Employer for $18-an-hour Employee

Paid time off (includes vacation time, personal time, sick leave, bereavement leave, jury duty)	Included in wages
Unemployment insurance	$ 0.18
Disability insurance	0.54
Social Security (FICA)/employer match	1.38
Workers compensation	1.10
Performance/bonus awards	0.15
Pension contribution	1.00
401K plan/employer match	0.48
Education-assistance plan	0.19
Training (on-the-job/seminars)	0.20
Parking/transportation subsidies	0.25
Employee discounts	0.07
Corporate support (payroll, human resources, administration, management, facilities, and other allocations)	0.76
Total benefits cost	$ 6.30
Total hourly cost including benefits	$ 24.30
Hourly cost of Super Temporary secretary	$ 20.00
You save	$ 4.30

viously, benefits will vary by company and state. It is hoped that you will be able to include factual information specific to your prospect's company's benefits policies and state regulations.

With this cost analysis in hand, the salesperson then can say, "You can see that the real cost of hiring a secretary from my temporary agency actually is *less* than hiring your own employee, and you don't have all of the liability. Our fixed hourly rate includes workers-compensation insurance, all withholdings, and other employee benefits that you, as an employer, would have to pay an employee."

If you have convinced your prospect that a temporary secretary costs $4.30 *less* an hour than a full-time secretary, and reiterate that all of the liability rests with you, the decision whether or not to use your company should be a pretty easy one to make. The prospect's reaction most likely will be, "When can you have one of your secretaries start?"

ANTICIPATE OBJECTIONS AHEAD OF TIME

The best way to handle objections is to anticipate what the objections will be and answer them *before* they are asked. "The best argument is that which seems merely an explanation," professed Dale Carnegie. The temporary secretarial service salesperson should have expected the prospect's objection and addressed the issue during the presentation.

Do not ignore an objection or dismiss an objection lightly. Neither should you accept the objection as a negative reality. Disarm prospects by acknowledging their concern and their need to know more. "Good point, Ed. Have you considered . . ." or "I'm glad you brought that up." And then answer the objection with your point of view. After giving your point of view, ask prospects what they think.

If that takes care of their questions, close the sale. If they have another question, handle their objections in the same way, and then close.

The Number-One Objection

The number-one objection usually is *price*. If a prospect feels that a product's or service's value doesn't exceed its cost, a salesperson should concentrate on heightening the desire of the prospect to increase the value of the product or service itself. If the direct approach fails, try offering a volume discount or scaled-down version of the product. If your prospect exclaims that your price has taken the product out of his or her allocated capital-expenditure budget, use the objection to close: Offer a rental or lease program. A monthly expense may not impact his or her capital-equipment budget at all.

If your price is higher than your competitor's price, acknowledge the fact enthusiastically. "Yes, our price is higher. Consider the fact that a Mercedes Benz costs more than a Ford." Then, state your reasons for selling your product at a higher price. There always are reasons to justify a higher price. In addition to features comparisons like bigger, better, louder, stronger, more durable, and perhaps self-cleaning, your product may have a higher resale value, or perhaps the demand for your product has driven the price up. It's the old supply-and-demand objection stopper.

The Second Most-Common Objection

Can you guess what the number-two objection is? "I don't need it." It's true, many times the prospect does not think he or she needs your product or service. If you are selling life insurance to a healthy thirty-year-old male, he may not see a need to buy your $100,000 life insurance policy. If you had a chart in your presentation that documents the number of accidental deaths that occur each year in his age bracket, however, he may pay more attention. Newspaper articles addressing the unfortunate deaths of numerous young men who died unexpectedly in auto accidents or because of heart attacks should be backup material. If an article talks about the plight of the young families left behind, all the better.

You should acknowledge the prospect's position of not recognizing an immediate need to buy life insurance, but then ask him to consider why buying an insurance policy *now* is a very intelligent thing to do. "You never will be able to buy life insurance at a lower price than today, because:

1. As you grow older, you get closer to the end of the mortality table and the cost per $1,000 of coverage goes up.

2. A whole-life insurance policy accumulates a cash value that you can borrow against, *and* in the event of your death, your family gets the full face value of insurance minus any outstanding loans.

3. If your alternative is to put extra cash (disposable income) into a savings account earning 8 percent interest, you should reconsider. If inflation is at 5 percent a year, you are losing 5 percent of the 8 percent interest your savings is earning. State and federal taxes take almost another 4 percent. The result is that after inflation and taxes, you actually *lose* 1 percent a year instead of earning 8 percent. That is a quick way to the poorhouse. Life insurance is the answer because you get protection at a low cost while you're young and cash value when you are older."

I have used the life-insurance example because it gives you a crystal-clear view of how to respond to the objection,

"I do not need your product right now." Of course, the prospect does need the insurance, and it is hoped that the three-point response will enable him or her to see why. Remember that an objection is just another way of telling you, the salesperson, to provide more information.

Let's look at one other "I do not need it" objection. You have just made a dynamic and comprehensive ten-minute presentation about your printing service. Your prospect promptly states that the last thing in the world she needs is another printing company. She already has one company printing her forms on NCR paper, another that prints her brochures and four-color artwork, and still another company printing her stationery and business cards.

Assuming you represent a full-service company, the prospect has just told you how to close her. By dealing with you, all of your prospect's printing can be done by one company. Your big advantage as your prospect's single source is that you can give her volume discounts on all of her purchases. The prospect only has to deal with one printer, and because of the volume of business she represents to your company, the prospect is a respected customer. (Of course, every customer gets the best from your company because your forward-thinking management knows that today's small customers are tomorrow's big customers.) Big customers can demand shorter lead times, better pricing, and other benefits that smaller customers normally cannot demand. Suggest that your prospective customer use her purchasing power with your company for just sixty days so that she may experience for herself the benefits of using a single printing source.

A SIMPLE MATTER OF EDUCATION

Handling objections is simply an educational process. If you have prequalified your prospects, there will almost always be a need for your product. I had one seminar attendee who sold copiers in Minneapolis jump up and say that such a statement is not true. Just two days earlier, he had called on a prospect who had just purchased a copier from a competitor, so obviously there was no need for his copy machine. How do you sell a copy machine to someone who just bought a copy machine? (And I thought he was going to ask a hard question!)

First of all, if he had done a better job prospecting, he would not have made the call in the first place. Or he would have made the call before the prospect purchased somebody else's copy machine. These were my own private thoughts, of course. What I actually said to the salesperson was, "You should have made your presentation anyway. If your prospect had purchased the other machine within the previous three days, he probably could legally return it, and you should encourage him to do so."

I know this may sound awful, but there is something wonderful about snatching a sale away from a competitor *after* she has spent her commission dollars! If the other machine was purchased for cash, sell the prospect on leasing so he can conserve precious working capital. Discount your machine if your competitor charges a restocking charge. Play up the benefits of your machine, and the more you talk, the more likely that your prospect will feel buyer's remorse. Yes, he made an unwise decision, but it wasn't his fault: The less-than-competent competitive salesperson simply did not give your prospect enough facts to make a pragmatic business decision.

Lack of money may be the only legitimate, acceptable reason why someone cannot buy your product. Even then, of course, you may offer rental, leasing, bank financing, trade allowance, and barter opportunities. Take your blinders off and *help* your prospect become a customer. It may be possible that a prospect really doesn't need your product. If you find this to be the case, acknowledge the fact and move on. It is hoped that the prospect will give you a few good leads at least.

LISTEN TO YOUR CUSTOMER AND RESPOND ENTHUSIASTICALLY

There are probably hundreds of objections that a prospect can voice before sending you on your way. By listening to your prospect, you soon will learn what his objections are. He may even tell you how to overcome his objections if you will simply master the art of listening. He probably will also communicate his objections to your competitor's products or services.

Even the most experienced salesperson can lose perspective and misread an objection as something personal. It's important to recognize that objections simply are one more logical step in the selling process. You must learn how to answer objections quickly, intelligently, and unemotionally.

Following are some of the most frequently heard objections and some suggested responses. After hearing an objection from a prospect, remember:

1. Always respond enthusiastically, not defensively.
2. Acknowledge your prospect's concern.
3. State your point of view.

Objection: *When we needed credit, your company turned us down.*

Response: I am glad that you brought that up. We have grown and your company has grown, and I think it's time to resubmit your application. You can count on me to pursue the credit limit you seek.

Objection: *Your predecessor sold us the wrong system.*

Response: I am confident that he believed that he matched your needs with an appropriate model. Sometimes, however, when insufficient information is collected, the result is an incorrect solution. I will make certain that it won't happen again.

Objection: *Your company has not been in business long enough.*

Response: Because we are a relatively new company, you should know that we are going to go the extra mile to meet your needs. We know how important it is to earn your respect and confidence. Together, our management team has more than 100 years of experience. Let me show you some testimonials from satisfied customers.

Objection: *Your product does not meet our specifications.*

Response: I am pleased that you brought that up. What do we have to do to get your business? Give me your order based on us meeting your specifications, and I will take it back to my management to see if we can comply.

Objection: *We only do business with local vendors.*

Response: I know how important it is to support local business and have vendors who can respond quickly. With your order, I will warehouse our product locally so that you can enjoy the same service as you would if we were locally based. Our warehouse business will help the local economy as well.

Objection: *Your competitor provides us with an entire system. We do not buy component parts.*

Response: Thank you for bringing that fact to my attention. I think you are in for a pleasant surprise. Compare the component prices against the cost of your system. I did a similar cost analysis for your competitor and saved him 24 percent off the system cost that his company had been incurring.

Objection: *We signed a two-year purchase agreement with your competitor.*
Response: Thank you for sharing that information with me. May I submit my bid now so that when your contractual obligation is behind you, you will be in a position to evaluate our product and price advantages? Who knows, if you see enough of a difference, you may be able to terminate early.

Objection: *You cannot provide a performance bond.*
Response: Even if we could, it would only serve to drive your costs up. Why not allow us to bill you incrementally as we complete segments of the total task? To give you a comfort zone, perhaps we can allow a penalty for late delivery.

Objection: *Our product evaluation committee turned your product down.*
Response: Who is on the evaluation committee? May I have the opportunity to make a group presentation? I have found that when given the opportunity to make such a presentation, I am able to very effectively handle any objections that members of the group may have.

Objection: *If you cannot meet our due date, we cannot do business.*
Response: We would not want to jeopardize the quality of our products by short-cycling the manufacturing process. Moreover, if we put your order in front of another customer's order, we would be showing

preferential treatment; we would not do that to you, and we cannot do that to the other customer. If immediate delivery is imperative, perhaps we could accommodate your request if you would be willing to pay a small overtime cost.

Objection: *We have a five-year relationship with our supplier, and I see no reason to change.*

Response: Thank you for sharing that with me. I know how difficult it is to change suppliers after so many years. Consider split-sourcing your needs. Simply give my firm a portion of the business and then compare the differences. You owe it to yourself to evaluate suppliers on a routine basis.

Objection: *Your company (product, you, or any combination of these) has a bad reputation. If I did business with you, it could cost me my job.*

Response: Thank you for bringing that to my attention. I believe that my company (product, etc.) is truly undeserving of such a reputation, but I'll be glad to address your concerns. With your permission, I can call any number of satisfied customers who will instantly dispel any negative impression you may have of my firm (or product, etc.). I'll also be happy to arrange for you to meet with my management to clear up any misunderstandings.

Objection: *Your competitor will give me free service, free attachments, etc.*

Response: I am pleased you brought that up. My competitor makes a fine product. We have priced our basic product so low, however, that we do not have that much room to play with the price. You only pay for the additional parts that you need and, of course, our standard service should be all that's necessary.

Objection: *We do not need any right now.*

Response: Thanks for sharing that information with me. When will you be purchasing this material again? To lock in today's price, you may want to consider ordering today because price increases normally are announced every quarter (six months, etc.).

CARDINAL RULES FOR HANDLING OBJECTIONS

1. Never say anything negative about your competitor.
2. Never say anything negative about your employer.
3. Never say anything negative about your product.
4. Never tell a customer he or she is wrong.
5. Never tell a customer that he or she does not understand.
6. Never argue with a customer.
7. Never lie to a customer, no matter what the circumstances. Long-term relationships are built on trust and integrity.
8. Never allow a customer to put you on the defensive.
9. Never lose your temper while with a customer.
10. Never say "I'm sorry," for it may subconsciously affect the positive way you see yourself. Use "I apologize" or "excuse me" instead.
11. Never let an objection go unanswered.
12. Always listen—*really listen*—to the objection.
13. Always acknowledge the objection and then state your point of view.
14. Always maintain a positive and enthusiastic attitude.
15. Always maintain good eye contact.
16. Always be prepared to prove your position with testimonials, reference sources, and corroborative documentation.
17. Always remember that objections are a natural part of the sales process and should not be considered a personal affront.

WORK ASSIGNMENT

Practice handling the following objections. Ask yourself how you would respond if your prospect said:

1. "I wouldn't do business with your company if it were the last company on earth!"
2. "I know you've been here five times to get this order. I just don't know. I can't make up my mind. I feel like you're rushing me."
3. "I need my boss's approval."
4. "It's a deal, but I have to pass it by my husband."
5. "The department head already has selected another fax machine."
6. "Your program is not cost effective."
7. "No, thanks. I'm not interested."
8. "If you can't provide me with financial statements, we just can't do business with you."
9. "I'll buy half from you and half from your competitor."
10. "Don't call me. I'll call you when we are ready to buy."

If you have experienced any difficulty responding, study this chapter until your responses to these typical objections become automatic. When you feel confident in your ability to handle objections, read on.

Of course, many objections really aren't objections at all. They are procrastination disguises. After responding to such an objection, try to close the sale. See Chapter 15, "The Ten Best Closing Techniques."

12
Networking Works

*"As I grow older, I pay less attention to what
men say. I just watch what they do."*

—Andrew Carnegie

There are scores of ways to sell your products or services.
You can make sales calls face-to-face or you can use telemarketing. You can implement a public-relations program
or a direct-mail campaign. You can advertise on television
or on the radio, or in newspapers or magazines. You can
sponsor a sports event, put discount coupons on cereal
boxes, or hire a pilot to skywrite your latest ad slogan.
Any or all of these efforts may be fruitful. One of the best
ways to effectively sell your product, however, is through
simple networking.

Networking groups can help you develop and use contacts, obtain inside information, share ideas, and lend support to other professionals. Even the briefest of encounters
can lead to a business deal. A salesperson can profit tremendously by associating with successful people in the
type of setting usually provided by networking.

SALES MEETINGS

Within your company, make the most of off-site company
retreats, company-sponsored social events, meeting

breaks, lunches, golf games, and other chances to network. Often you'll find that getting to know the right people at work is at least as important as doing an outstanding job. Sales meetings provide the perfect forum for networking.

The goal of any sales meeting must be to make every salesperson take action and create change. Meetings can improve communication and enhance participation in making decisions, provide immediate feedback to opinions, improve team spirit, and optimally, create synergy as the group becomes more than the sum of its parts.

Meetings can be unproductive for a number of reasons, such as:

1. No agenda
2. Meeting objectives not communicated
3. Lack of leadership and control
4. Lack of proper planning
5. Failure of those attending to present their ideas clearly and concisely
6. Time wasted on discussing "why" something is rather than how to change it
7. Improper use of audiovisual aids

Before you call or attend any meeting, you should know its specific purpose. A memo or agenda distributed well in advance of the meeting is the best way to focus everyone on the purpose of any meeting and make the meeting more productive. The agenda should be a brief, written statement of the objectives, the issues to be discussed, the times the meeting will begin and end, the meeting location, the participants, and the preparation required of the attendees. If you are attending a sales meeting and have not received an agenda, call and request one.

The meeting chairperson establishes the atmosphere of the meeting and sets its parameters. He or she must start and end the meeting on time and maintain the meeting's pace. The chairperson keeps the meeting on track by directing the discussion according to the agenda and acts as facilitator to make sure that the meeting objectives are met.

A sales meeting provides a wonderful opportunity to learn and network. If the meeting is at your home office, use every spare minute to talk to other salespeople and inquire about their successes and failures. Use the occasion to meet the support staff you talk to all year-round but never have met in person. Your relationship with them probably will improve once you really know each other.

Brainstorming sessions and group assignments are great opportunities to get everyone involved. While I wholeheartedly support interactive sales training, I have seldom found role-playing to be very effective in regional meetings, although it certainly has its place in a basic selling course or perhaps with newly hired salespeople. Probably a better use of time for experienced, professional salespeople is discussing products and services, industry trends, competition, financing, and operational information. Management should review and compare past sales campaigns with current sales campaigns, discuss the company's future plans, announce new compensation programs, and present outstanding achievement awards.

The regional or national sales meeting is the time and place to find out how much latitude you have. Sometimes I don't know which is more difficult, selling the customer or the home office! Many times I would take advantage of a sales opportunity only to have someone in the home office refuse to accept my order simply because the customer wanted something out of the ordinary. Many systems are so stringent that if you change one condition, it throws everything off. For example, a travel agency has the latitude to discount the price of an airline ticket out of the commission the airline pays them. I doubt that an airline representative would discount the price of an airline ticket directly to the customer. If the representative did, he or she would infuriate travel agents. Different businesses have different rules that are unique to their industries. Find out what is acceptable to your industry and how much flexibility you have.

A sales meeting should have a specific time set aside for department heads to discuss important issues with the sales force. Make up a list of questions and unresolved issues, and take the list to the meeting with you. Which departments are not supporting you and your customers? Is customer service taking care of your customers? A customer may be able to live with certain small problems, while other problems can cost you new sales and repeat business. How do your customers rate service and maintenance on equipment after the sale? Is the accounting department billing correctly? Is your training department doing its job? How about advertising and quality control? Perhaps problems are beyond the scope of a department's charter, resources, or level of competence. Do not go home until your questions are answered and any unresolved issues are addressed.

Many sales meetings, however well intentioned, end up failing because too much nonprogrammed time is allowed. You should not adjourn at 4:30 P.M. and expect all of your sellers visiting from out of town to be able to function fully at 8:00 A.M. the following day. Perhaps 10 percent will show up bright and chipper the next day but 75 percent will be holding up their alcohol-soaked brains with both hands. No matter what you present, their bloodshot eyes will not see it. If they are able to see whatever you are presenting, they probably won't be able to assimilate it. About 12 percent will arrive late because they needed an extra hour to give the aspirin a chance to work on their hangovers. The remaining 3 percent simply will be unaccounted for.

Make every minute at a sales meeting count. Not only does the employer have the expense of the facilities, food, transportation, and material costs, but the sales manager is losing a certain amount of productivity by taking everyone out of the field. Keep the meeting concise, encourage interaction, and control the leisure time. Give the attendees assignments to complete for the following morning's session. Ask each salesperson to write a two-page analysis of his or her toughest sale or biggest sale. As the statements are read the following day, each salesperson will learn from the experiences of his or her colleagues. Have the attendees write opening statements to get a customer's attention. Prepare a quiz on the company's newest product to see whose product knowledge is up-to-date. To extend the business meeting into the evening, cater dinner in a meeting room. A buffet probably will be less expensive than what it would cost for everyone to eat in a restaurant.

Despite all of these precautions, the sales manager still may wake up with a fire hose under his hotel door. His wife still may find an article of female clothing that was placed in his luggage by some of his salespeople. Some poor waiter probably will be pushed into the swimming pool twice in one night. But other than a few minor disturbances, your sales meeting should be a success.

NETWORK WHILE YOU TRAVEL

When you're on the road, by all means take advantage of the occasion to establish a wide network of contacts in every type of profession. Traveling allows you to schedule networking time into your itinerary. If you are going to a trade show, find out ahead of time from the meeting planner if there are any activities formally or informally scheduled. If not, plan your own, whether that means setting up a hospitality suite or arranging to take a group to dinner. Find out what associations are located in the city you're visiting and evaluate the potential for networking. Renew the friendships and relationships of existing contacts who'll also be in attendance.

INDUSTRY OPPORTUNITIES

Keep up with who's who in your industry by reading trade journals and joining industry organizations. Become active in civic and professional organizations, and volunteer to serve on their committees and task forces to increase your visibility.

If your industry holds regional or national trade conventions, attend as many as is cost effective. Under one roof, you'll find exhibitors from all over the country and, perhaps, from all over the world. Take advantage of all of the networking opportunities a trade show or exposition offers. Really work the convention floor by going from one exhibitor to the next. A smart advertising sales representative at the *San Francisco Business Times* attends just about every business convention at the George R. Moscone Convention Center. She walks from booth to booth, talking to individuals and handing out business-to-business advertising brochures and rate cards. This is networking at its finest.

Your company might sponsor a wine-and-cheese party at the end of the day, a very appropriate social selling opportunity. It's a great way to say "hello" to old customers and meet new prospects after standing on the convention floor all day and attending technical, industry-oriented meetings. Oftentimes, you will find all of the salespeople huddled together in one part of the room while the prospects socialize among themselves. Spread out and "work" the party.

Introduce yourself to those attending. "How are you enjoying the convention? Are you familiar with our company and its products?" If an attendee is already a customer, ask who his or her account representative is, and if the representative is in attendance, seat the two together. If the sales representative is not attending, introduce the customer to some of the other individuals in the room. Every salesperson should agree to do the same for each other. If your company sends more than one salesperson to a trade show, make sure that all of you attend seminars and workshops separately, so that each salesperson can speak to as many people as time permits in order to cover the trade show thoroughly.

Limit your intake of alcohol to very little, or better yet, drink nothing at all at these company functions. Remember that you are working, and you should want to take full advantage of this great opportunity to network and meet new prospects. Keep circulating and be sure to introduce yourself. If you want to negotiate a sale or discuss an issue at length with any one prospect, set up a breakfast meeting for the next morning, or arrange another convenient meeting time during the convention. If one person tries to monopolize your time, graciously excuse yourself and keep circulating.

A very bright salesperson who sold cardiac monitoring systems to hospitals made a six-figure income by following a cardiology convention around the United States. In each new location at a hotel near the convention, he would sponsor a hospitality suite that he would promote prior to the convention. His networking brought him in contact with physicians and hospital personnel from all over the world who purchased his electronic cardiac monitoring equipment.

Trade shows can be great places to find qualified sales leads, learn what the competition is doing, and conduct a little market research. If time and your company's budget permit, be an exhibitor. Most trade or industry publications include calendars of upcoming events and should list exposition information specific to your field. Call or write to the trade show management or contact listed to request convention information that should provide you with statistics about previous shows' attendance figures, a list of attendees, and information on being an exhibitor. Ask associates if they've participated in the shows in which you're interested. Find out if your company has been a past exhibitor in any of the shows. If so, were the company's goals met? How worthwhile was the experience? Did anyone identify the business that resulted from these shows to find out if the expenditures were cost justified?

If your company wants to participate as an exhibitor, make sure that specific, measurable goals are developed and agreed on before you send in the application and related fees. Take the time to investigate the possibility of product tie-ins with other companies that may be interested in exhibiting their products or services. To make decisions about booth size and to negotiate a good location, to decide what products will be displayed and ensure their prompt delivery, to make sure you're listed in the exposition directory, to design the booth, to develop the signs, and to promote the exhibit, you'll need to *begin planning at least six months ahead*. It's important that you make sure that your top sellers are available to staff the booth rather than risk damaged credibility and potential loss of sales with a less-than-superlative sales group. Creating a good impression still is paramount, even when you're surrounded by the din and confusion of a trade show.

Your booth space, booth design, number of sellers attending, travel and entertainment expenses, shipping costs, and promotional activities will depend largely on your company's budget. The average cost to build an exhibit (which frequently is used for more than one show) is about $15,700. The National Convention and Visitors Bureau reports that the average cost per delegate to a convention is $977; this figure includes lodging, food, and transportation. Shipping costs will vary depending on your product. Exhibit space costs approximately $14.50 per square foot according to the Trade Show Bureau, and the smallest unit of space available usually is 100 square feet.

To increase the foot traffic to your booth and the chance for greater sales, promote your exhibit to prospects and customers in a company newsletter or direct-mail piece *before* the show. Your sales goals should, in large part, determine your promotion budget. Trade shows offer tremendous opportunities for making contacts with potential prospects. Listen to what trade-show attendees tell you about your product or service. You can get invaluable feedback on what's good and what's not-so-good, along with suggestions for product improvement or service after the sale.

You'd be surprised at how often salespeople forget the main reason why they came to the trade show: to sell. Focus the bulk of your attention on those attendees who are at the show because they want to buy what you're selling. The Trade Show Bureau reports that, on average, approximately 61 percent of any show's attendees are planning a purchase, while 84 percent have buying power. Unfortunately, only 17 percent of the attendees later are contacted by sales personnel.

You must have a precise method for separating the real prospects who've stopped by your booth from the browsers. After the show, pursue real prospects with a telephone call or letter and sales materials, but do it no later than ten to fifteen days after the show. Even browsers should be contacted, though such follow-ups are less urgent than follow-ups of real prospects and should be prioritized accordingly.

Several sources of trade-show information are listed in Resources at the end of the book.

SEMINARS

Do you want to make group presentations to 500 people two times a month at a presentation cost per person of less than $0.48 instead of the national average of $239 per individual sales call? Would you like to have your prospect's undivided attention for three hours? Would you like to establish yourself as an authority in your industry? Would you like to increase your sales by 100 times? If your answer is "yes" to one or more of these questions, read the next part of the chapter very carefully.

Smart sales professionals have been using the seminar forum to sell their products and services for many years. In biblical times, spice merchants used the seminar format to teach prospects how to cook with the new spices. They could answer questions and deliver their products on the spot.

Seminars may be just the right sales vehicle for you. If you are selling a diaper service, you may want to consider holding seminars for expectant and new mothers. For your guest speaker, invite a psychologist who'll talk about the psychological impact of bringing home a new baby. A local baby furniture retail store owner may want to discuss the necessities involved in furnishing the baby's room. You could invite a physician to talk about prenatal and new-born care. Of course, his or her endorsement on the use of cloth diapers would be a tremendous plus.

As each attendee enters the meeting room, she will find your diaper service brochure on her chair. It may be difficult to dissuade a new mother from using disposable diapers, but you can spend a serious amount of time on the adverse effects on the environment that result from using disposable diapers. Show photographs of disposable diapers in a landfill and include copies of newspaper articles reporting the decline in disposable-diaper usage and the renewed popularity of cloth diapers.

Very few products and services are not suitable for seminars. An attendee at one of my new business seminars said that he was a private detective and did not believe that he could sell his services at a seminar. I heartily disagreed and pointed out that his services could *best* be sold in a seminar setting. I asked him whether or not he had a specialty, and he responded that he worked on embezzlement cases one day, corporate fraud the next, and basically accepted every client that walked through his door. He said that he was especially good at locating missing persons. He could even find people who did not know they were lost! Using medical records, school records, bank records, motor-vehicle records, occupational records, relatives, governmental agencies, and a host of other sources, he found six out of ten people that he was trying to locate. He really enjoyed that part of his work.

I suggested that he hold seminars for people who want to find someone. Creditors want to locate debtors; bail bondsmen want to locate clients who have jumped bail; parents want to locate runaway juveniles; and adopted children may want to locate their birth parents. Why not target individuals in these and other specific markets by advertising a seminar to find out how an expert locates someone?

As the host, the private detective would bring a computer and demonstrate how the various programs and reporting agencies could be accessed. Such a seminar would establish the host as an expert. He could review a few cases and walk the attendees through the different processes that he uses to locate a person.

Most of the attendees are not going to attempt to find someone on their own. After the seminar, they will realize that they need access to special kinds of reporting services that are available to the private detective. After two or three hours, chances are great that the attendees will be intrigued and impressed with the scope of the host's knowledge. He has spent his time more efficiently than if each attendee had come individually to his office and he had listened to each one's problem before discussing his services. In individual office consultations, the detective could not possibly convey his worth as well as and to as great an extent as he could in a seminar.

Six months after our meeting, the private detective was conducting two seminars a month throughout the western United States. Not only was he earning good money from his seminar fees, but his investigation business had tripled in revenues for most attendees decided to hire an authority rather than attempt to locate someone on their own.

Yes, most products and services can be sold in a seminar setting. Make your seminar more interesting by inviting guest lecturers who complement your subject. For example, if you are selling furniture, invite a well-known interior decorator. If you are selling construction financing, invite a major builder who uses your services. An oil and gas company could invite oil and gas association directors and government officials. The less known you or your company are, the more you need credible lecturers to help you draw a large crowd. You may think it is difficult to sell microwave ovens, ice-making machines, or veterinarian services in a seminar setting, but if you can use your imagination and marketing skills, you can find a unique approach.

NETWORK MARKETING

Word-of-mouth advertising is unquestionably the greatest form of advertising. It costs little, if any, money, and yet it offers one of the best opportunities to turn prospects into happy customers. Word-of-mouth endorsements are viewed as unbiased and more credible than regular media ads. Anticipation of product efficacy is high, and that normally means many sales.

Once someone buys something, he or she usually defends the purchase. Each of us likes to believe that he or she has made a sound decision when he or she has done the proper homework, shopped around, or negotiated a good deal. As a result, each of us likes to affirm that his or her selection is correct by sharing the good news with anyone who will listen.

If, on the other hand, someone purchases something that does not quite meet expectations, or that later he or she is disappointed by, then the person may be reluctant to broadcast the fact that he or she is not a shrewd buyer. Many people refrain from contacting law-enforcement agencies about suffering losses at the hands of con artists because they are afraid of appearing foolish. So what does all of this have to do with networking? Many sales professionals do all of their prospecting while networking. If you know how and where to network, you can multiply your sales.

The champion networkers probably are the home-party sales forces. Simply put, a distributor invites friends, neighbors, and coworkers to come over after dinner one evening for coffee and dessert. The group receives an informal, brief presentation on the product of the evening, which could be anything from cosmetics to sexy lingerie. The evening is light and fun, and significant sales are made. Most important, each attendee is asked to hold a party in his or her home. Each attendee has a powerful sphere of influence, for neighbors, friends, coworkers, and any relatives who live in the area may be perfect prospects to invite. Of course, the host or hostess receives a special discount on his or her purchases. This is networking at its finest. Ask the management of Amway or Mary Kay Cosmetics about how wonderful network marketing can be.

If you sign up people to sell under you, you receive an override (sales commission) on each of their sales. If you enlist ten people, and they each sign up ten people, you conceivably could have thousands of people working for you in no time at all. For real impact, I'll illustrate that for you.

NUMBER OF PEOPLE SELLING FOR YOU

You sign up 10 people	10
Each of them signs up 10 people	100
Each of them signs up 10 people	1,000
Each of them signs up 10 people	10,000
Each of them signs up 10 people	100,000

After awhile, of course, you theoretically would run out of people! The lesson here is, in short, that networking *works*. Why sell to one person when you can sell to 100, or 1,000, or even 100,000 people? One salesperson makes a sale for his one-day seminar after a two-hour sales presentation to a potential customer. The salesperson feels great; after all, he just earned a $200 commission! Another seminar salesperson produces a half-hour infomercial. She persuades a local television station manager to air it on a per-inquiry basis on late-night television. The first airing of the tape produces 300 sales, and after expenses the salesperson puts $60,000 in her pocket!

The only real differences between the two approaches is that one salesperson addresses a smaller audience once, while the other speaks to a much larger audience, the members of which may be exposed to her message more than once. Do not talk to one prospect if you can talk to 10, 1,000, or 1,000,000. Use satisfied customers to bring in more customers. For instance, at the end of each seminar, the salesperson asks each attendee to provide a list of five people who, in their opinion, would benefit by attending the same seminar. That is networking.

Do you sell a product or service that lends itself to home-party selling or seminars?

SOCIAL SELLING

Social selling is a contradiction in terms. Social implies convivial activities or being fond of the company of others. Selling, on the other hand, means to exchange ownership of a product or service for money, or barter for something of equal value. Social selling really is just a relationship building tool. Whenever clients are away from their routines, the chances of being influential are significant. A great deal of business is discussed on the golf course. Companies buy cabins with views of beautiful lakes for use by their customers (and sales staff) who enjoy fishing. Prospects are entertained on yachts, at ballparks, and on cruises.

How do you compete with a competitor who is taking your prospect to a private country club to play golf? Imagine having a prospect at a corporate lakeside cabin for a four-day weekend, or taking him fishing for marlin in the Gulf of Mexico for three days. If the prospect wants to be invited again next year, he probably is going to favor your competitor's product or service, even if it is not necessarily the best product or service at the best price.

However well the prospect intends to perform his duties and responsibilities with integrity, he is undermining you, your company, or your product or service. He may argue that your company has not been in business long enough. He may contend that a change of sources would be too troublesome for his firm at this time. He may hang his denial hat on an insignificant feature that his yacht-owning supplier's product has that yours does not have. In short, if he wants or needs to justify why he should do business with one supplier instead of another supplier, he will do it.

Many companies specifically forbid employees to receive gifts from and be entertained by suppliers because they want unbiased, pragmatic purchasing decisions that serve the company's best interest, not the employees'. In many instances, people placed in positions of great authority have been terminated for violating their fiduciary responsibility by placing themselves in compromising positions. Never pay someone to give you an order. If you can buy them, so can your competitor. If you strike up a friendship with a client and decide to go fishing together, have a great time, but share the expenses just as you would with any other friend. Your prospect/friend will respect your integrity and he will not find himself compromised.

Sell your product or service on its own merits, on its strengths and benefits. If your company owns a yacht, season tickets to a baseball or football team in your city, or a cabin in the mountains, let others in your company use these assets to entertain politicians or bankers. You wouldn't want a vice president of purchasing firing the purchasing agent and blackballing your company. Leave that unpleasant experience for your competitors.

If you find yourself at a party or in a social setting with a customer, be yourself. But realize that you shouldn't relax too much. Such a setting may allow the customer to share some inside information with you or give you her view on your company. Just sit back and listen. But remember, it's not the right time to try to close a sale.

THE NITTY-GRITTY OF NETWORKING

Many organizations are made up of members who, in addition to any other benefit the organization may offer, want to network. At a recent Rotary Club meeting, I met a local banker, an insurance agent, an attorney, a pharmacist, a local printer, and an auto dealer. Each regarded me as a potential client, and I regarded each of them as a potential client. When I was asked to give a short talk about my company, I jumped at the chance to sell 100 local businesspeople at one time.

When giving a lecture or attending an affair where you expect to meet potential customers, be prepared to take advantage of the networking opportunities. Take plenty of business cards with you. Write pertinent information about each individual on the back of the card you collect from him or her. Eat before you go to the affair, so you won't be tempted to waste valuable networking time eating and drinking.

Most important, attempt to qualify your prospects as you circulate. Find out if your potential customer needs what you sell. If so, exchange cards and set up an appointment. If not, continue to circulate. Can he afford your product or service? Asking about his budget is perfectly acceptable. Lastly, ask yourself: Why would he want to buy from me?

If you are attending a bankers' conference and you sell drive-up teller windows, you are not going to waste too much time with an attorney who, like you, is networking. You won't spend too much time with a banker who has no budget for your product or with one who already has equipped his bank and branches with drive-up windows. You will continue to circulate until you find the banker who needs and can afford drive-up windows and who perhaps did not know who to talk to until you came along. Exchange business cards, set up an appointment, and keep circulating.

When circulating, introduce yourself and simply ask your fellow attendee what company she works for and what her position is with her company. Then volunteer the same information in return. Weave your qualifying questions into the conversation. *Remember: Do not attempt to sell your product or service at a social event.* There will be plenty of time to close your prospect later.

The keys to profitable networking at an event are to circulate and to listen. Do not assert yourself too much, but do not be afraid to make your presence known.

One accountant introduced himself to me at a business luncheon that we both attended several years ago. At the time, I was not pleased with the accountant I had so I eventually gave my business to the assertive accountant who introduced himself to me at the luncheon. I also bought a copy machine from one of my seminar attendees. And the gentleman who now is my dentist attended one of my seminars several years ago.

Networking works if you know how to seize the opportunities it presents. For instance, if you belong to the Rotary Club or another civic or affinity group, don't hesitate to offer a discount to members, if applicable. The discount is justified by the potential quantity the group as a whole will buy.

No matter what you sell, sooner or later networking opportunities will arise whether by design or happenstance. If you never overlook the chance to network, the rewards will come and you probably will have fun at the same time! And, by all means, follow the cardinal rule in maintaining your network: Keep your telephone and mailing lists up-to-date!

13
Can You Make Stone Soup?

*"Synergistic salespeople do not just sell
products. They sell participation."*

An American soldier was very hungry and so tired that he
could hardly raise his hand to knock on the door. After
fighting a five-day battle, he had walked nearly seventy-
five miles through the French countryside to a small village of perhaps forty or fifty homes. An angry woman
opened the door and demanded to know the nature of his
business. He told her of his circumstances and asked for a
piece of bread, a glass of water, or anything that she could
spare. She screamed at him to go away, saying that she
could hardly feed herself as she angrily slammed the door
in his face.

The solider then walked to a second house, where he
again asked for food or water. The owner refused his
requests in a manner that was even less understanding
than that of the woman in the first house.

So the soldier walked a bit farther until his gaze fell on
a small town square in the middle of which he discovered
a cracked but nevertheless functioning water fountain.

The soldier drank as much water as his stomach could hold and, in the middle of the park, started a small fire over which he placed the shell of his helmet that he had filled with water. Inside the helmet, he placed two average-sized stones and began stirring the mixture.

A little boy approached the soldier and asked what he was doing. The soldier replied, "I am making the most delicious stone soup in the whole world." The boy asked if he could have some. "Certainly," the soldier replied, "but the soup needs a few vegetables to make it really delicious." The boy exclaimed that his parents had a few carrots at home. As the child hurriedly ran home for the carrots, a married couple entered the park and asked the soldier what he was doing. "I'm making the most delicious stone soup in the whole world." The couple asked the soldier if he would share his bounty with them. He replied, "Of course, but I need a soup bone and perhaps some spices to make this soup the very best." The wife explained that she'd rush home to find something to contribute to the mixture. An old woman passing through the park stopped to inquire about the soldier's concoction and helped the mixture by adding a few potatoes. After one hour, there were several more people who had contributed whatever ingredients they had on hand to the soup.

At just the right moment, the soldier removed the stones and ladled out a cup of marvelous stone soup to each person who had contributed ingredients. There still was plenty of soup left over for the starving soldier to enjoy.

In this children's story, the soldier is the catalyst who brings these individuals together for their mutual gain. None of those who enjoyed the delicious soup had the ingredients to make the soup individually. The soldier's ingenuity brought everyone together for the common good. This illustrates synergism at its best.

THE WHOLE IS MORE THAN THE
SUM OF ITS PARTS

Synergistic selling is one of the techniques used by most highly successful salespeople. Synergistic selling may be one of the best-kept secrets in business. Without the use of this wonderful sales technique, our soldier may have starved to death. Without the use of synergistic selling techniques, you may not achieve the sales goals you've set for yourself. Few sales accomplishments are more gratifying than making good stone soup, because you make it possible for many people to enjoy the benefits of a larger group endeavor through small, individual contributions.

Synergistic selling is like a potluck family picnic. Each member of the family brings one prepared dish, but eats from all of the dishes at dinnertime. How can you use this concept to sell your product or service? You can do what our highly successful saleswoman did and start a cooperative to purchase business forms. Because of the group's purchasing power, it receives larger discounts than would be available to any individual business member.

EVERYBODY MUST WIN

Many country clubs charge their members a fixed amount of money for food each month whether they use the club's dining facilities or not. The clubs do this because it virtually guarantees an income stream with which the country club can cover its fixed expenses. This is great for the club because it guarantees member patronage. It also is great for the members who eat at the club because they're consequently guaranteed the services of an excellent chef and good service by the staff. The only losers in this scenario are the members who do not eat at the club but who still have to pay to subsidize those who do. This is not an example of synergistic sales, because someone loses. The ideal sales strategy does not allow for such exploitation.

Synergistic selling is creating a system that allows all the parties to benefit by the association. It may be as simple as enabling a number of departments or people within one organization to benefit by the joint efforts or purchases of the whole.

As a youngster, I worked on my Aunt Mary Louise's farm during the summer months. We baled hay, planted vegetables, picked cucumbers, and generally worked very hard. In retrospect, the pickle company in town was one of the best synergistic sales organizations I've witnessed. The company provided the farmers with seeds and fertilizer. At harvest time, it bought the cucumbers (less any advances) and sold the pickles to packagers all over North America. By doing business this way, everybody won—the farmer, the packagers, the consumers, and, of course, the pickle company itself.

OK, let's imagine that you are selling toothbrushes and need a specific synergistic selling technique. Remember the old adage, "Give a man a fish, feed him for a day; teach him how to fish, feed him for a lifetime"? Give lectures to high school students about proper dental hygiene, and give them sample toothbrushes in addition to your brochures. Encourage frequent checkups with a dentist, and give the dentist a supply of your toothbrushes to give to his or her patients.

Within a few months, your sales should begin to soar. Students will tell their parents and siblings what you taught them, showing them your brochure and toothbrush. And you'll receive an implied endorsement from the dentist because he or she is distributing free samples for you. The next time someone buys, they will more than likely reach for the toothbrush they've been using—yours. The school receives a free service, the students receive instruction on how to keep their teeth and gums healthy, the local dentist's business picks up, and you sell more products. With synergistic selling, everyone wins.

If you are selling automobiles, you may want to consider approaching companies in your area and offering a corporate discount. Once approved (and who can reject a corporate discount to all employees?), you can distribute one-sided, black-and-white fliers that announce to each employee that he or she is entitled to a $500 discount on any Toyota purchased during the month of January. Highlight the fact that this is a special offer available only to company employees. Make similar arrangements with credit unions, civic or fraternal organizations, churches, or any affinity groups in your area. Contact charitable organizations and offer to donate $500 to their charities for every contributor who buys a car during the month of February.

If you offered a discount on all Toyotas, for example, to customers of the Easy Come Easy Go Bank, everyone involved would benefit. The bank would be giving its customers added value because their customers would not be getting a discount on your automobiles if they banked elsewhere. And the bank's customers would benefit because they would receive something of value for simply banking at the Easy Come Easy Go Bank. You would be amazed by how many people select one bank over another because they receive a portable radio, alarm clock, or discounted airline tickets for simply opening an account. Bankers would be the first to tell you that premium offers work. If a customer wants to finance the automobile purchase, the bank may consider a special automobile loan rate to add additional value to your discount offer. You will sell lots of cars, and your distributorship's earnings will climb off the charts.

Contact the local, independent car insurance offices and

negotiate a discount deal with them for their customers. Offer to write a few paragraphs in their newsletters about the best ways to buy a car.

Give all the members of a local country club a discount on the purchase of all Toyotas bought during September. You may want to offer a standard discount of $500 to all members, with an additional $100 discount for any member who brings in a golf scorecard under 75.

How can an accountant, attorney, or physician use synergistic selling? As their businesses become more competitive every year, professionals must market their services more effectively. This is a great opportunity for sales professionals as the challenge to maintain their market share begins to accelerate.

Accountants, attorneys, or physicians could provide their customers and potential customers with newsletters that advise and inform them about current trends, new technology, and new laws that may affect the consumer. What are the benefits of such a newsletter? It would establish the accountant, attorney, or physician professionally not only as an authority on the subject matter but as someone who cares about the welfare of his or her clients. It would keep his or her name in front of the customer base and entice new clients and patients. A professional could write his or her own newsletter, or could use a company such as Friedman & Associates in Chicago, Illinois, to do it for them. Irwin Friedman, CPA, can be reached at 401 North Michigan Avenue, Chicago, IL 60611-4240, (312) 245-1666.

Professionals could hold educational seminars in their offices. They could start their own referral services. I know one enterprising physician who recorded five-minute audiotapes on the illnesses that most often afflict mankind, such as diabetes, heart disease, AIDS, cancer, influenza, migraine headaches, backaches, and cataracts. He arranged for a 900-number telephone service in his geographical area. His income immediately rose because people recently diagnosed with any of these maladies called the 900 number to hear the appropriate tape, and paid $1 a minute for five minutes. At the end of the tape, the operator captured the caller's name, address, and telephone number, ensuring that every caller was placed on the newsletter mailing list. After paying the cost of the telephone services, the physician earned $2.50 per call, he developed a wonderful list of potential patients, and his patient census grew to a point where he had to bring in three physician partners in one year. He knew the value of synergistic selling.

No matter what your product or service, develop a way to wrap your product or service around other products, and package your sale. Whether you are selling computers, baby carriages, diaper services, copier services, or stone soup, the concept works. How can you use synergistic selling in your selling effort?

FIND THE RECIPE FOR STONE SOUP

If the hungry soldier had resigned himself to sit in the park and wait for something to happen, he surely would have died of hunger. Rather than hoping that opportunity would knock on his door, he devised a plan and carried it out to final execution. Use the same process to increase your sales. (In fact, the most valued secret to sales success is a related, but even smarter, approach. If you can't guess what it is, you will find the answer in Chapter 20.)

Synergistic selling works, so take the initiative. Take your product to the market with exciting and novel propositions and become a world-renowned "stone-soup chef." Can't you almost smell it?

WORK ASSIGNMENT

Write a synergistic marketing plan for your product or service. If you do not have a product or service, write a few paragraphs about how you would synergistically sell a landscaping service. How would you bring the nursery, wholesalers, distributors, home owners, city agencies, and others together to increase your landscaping business?

14
The Most Miraculous
Selling Strategy

*"A good salesperson should be able to sell two
pairs of trousers with a burial suit."*

—Unknown

The president of a $10-million security guard company
was more than a little concerned about his corporate problems. He needed answers to his prayers and solutions to
his problems. One of his security guards had recently shot
an unarmed man outside a bank in downtown Los Angeles. Another one of his guards was caught by the Los
Angeles police stealing a customer's equipment at three
o'clock in the morning. As arrests by his guards were
increasing, so were the company's workers-compensation
claims. He had two false-arrest lawsuits pending. To reduce theft at the facilities of special customers such as
high-technology research and development contractors,
government facilities, and defense contractors, he brought
in police dogs to guard the outer perimeters. Unfortunately, a prominent scientist was viciously attacked by one
of the guard dogs and had to be hospitalized for two weeks
after undergoing major plastic surgery on his face and
neck.

As if all of that were not enough, the president had to find a way to reduce his overtime cost. The president actually would earn more than $1 million a year if he reduced his overhead by eliminating the overtime cost. At the rate of $1 million annually, the overtime costs would drive him out of business.

Desperate, he looked up business consultants in the yellow pages, found one or two consultants who advertised the experience he sought, and also telephoned a few friends for referrals. One business associate recommended one of the consultants the president had selected out of the yellow pages, so he contacted that consultant and made an appointment for the same afternoon.

The consultant listened carefully to all of the president's problems and took copious notes. Suffering from nervous exhaustion and sheer frustration with his mounting difficulties, the president finally stopped talking and waited for a response from the consultant.

The consultant picked up the telephone and called the Los Angeles Police Department (LAPD) and inquired about the shooting. Indeed, the guard had shot an unarmed man outside the bank. The police ran a check on the unarmed man and found an arrest warrant on him for felonious escape from a Virginia penitentiary. Furthermore, there were at least ten witnesses who signed eyewitness reports that the shooting was provoked by the unarmed man, and the guard was justified in shooting him. In fact, the LAPD intended to issue a letter of commendation to the guard and his employer.

As it turned out, the guard who was caught stealing equipment at 3:00 A.M. was merely delivering diagnostic instruments to a surgeon who had asked to have them brought over to his office. Because the doctor needed them by 9:00 A.M., the guard was loading the instruments into his trunk during his work shift, and, in fact, intended to deliver the instruments on his own time. The slightly embarrassed arresting officer apologized to both the security guard and the doctor.

The consultant recommended to the company president that all the guards attend special self-defense classes and physical-conditioning programs to minimize the likelihood of personal injuries occurring on the job and to decrease the corresponding workers-compensation claims. The consultant also urged that the guards stop making arrests. He recommended that the guards observe and report all suspicious behavior to the police and let the police actually arrest any and all suspects.

The consultant also suggested that the firm use its guard dogs as the police do in K-9 cars. A dog should be used only when a known assailant must be located in areas too dangerous for guards to go. The president's general-liability insurance policy probably covered the expenses related to the "dog bites scientist" incident. The consultant reminded the president that there may be some recourse against the company that trained the guard dog, and the company that hired the security company may have a general-liability policy as well.

The consultant even managed to solve the problem of escalating overtime costs by rearranging the hours and numbers of days each security guard worked, and managed to do so in compliance with state wage-and-hour laws.

The president's eyes lit up as he felt his burden being lifted and the black cloud over his head disappearing. In less than one hour, a great business consultant had given him concrete answers and solutions.

The consultant recommended an additional ten hours of consulting time so that he could analyze all areas of opportunities and other problems the security guard company faced. He wanted his attorney to review the company's labor practices for legal compliance. The consultant wanted his accountant to create weekly profit-and-loss statements for the guard service, so that the president could manage his business better. Surely there were many cost centers and marketing opportunities that should be explored. Perhaps the president should be renting uniforms instead of buying them, or maybe his guards should be buying their own uniforms and receiving clothing allowances. How was the firm recruiting its employees? The company's benefits program needed review as did many other areas.

What did the consultant do for his own company? He expanded a one-hour business consultation into a ten-hour contract, opened the door for a multitude of additional services, and earned referral fees from his accountant and benefits specialist. As these professionals complete their work and uncover other problem areas, the consultant will be needed to deal with those issues as well. Yes, perhaps it's a tad incestuous, but it works, and *everybody wins.*

FORM A SALES "PARTNERSHIP"

A sales professional should be a consultant. No matter what you sell, you probably know more about your product or service than your prospective customers. When you make a sales call, during the probing process ask your prospect about her goals and her needs. You are trying to identify problems so that you can offer your product as a solution. As you help the customer and she buys your product, you really are forming a sales *partnership.*

Put yourself in the role of an adviser. How can you solve your potential customer's problem? Sometimes customers don't even know they have problems until you educate them. Customers want to be reassured, however, that your product or service will satisfy the needs of their companies. How do you convince them that they need you and your product, particularly if they have never purchased your product or used your services before?

Develop a survey that will position you as a consultant. The survey could ask your customers questions such as: How long have they been customers? Do they want to continue doing business with you in the future? How do they rate your product? How do they rate your service after the sale? How do they rate you in terms of follow-up during the past sixty days?

Put together a desktop presentation book (similar to the one discussed in Chapter 9) that contains actual surveys completed by your customers that you can show your prospects. If you have a couple of surveys that are less than complimentary, make sure you have rectified the problem and have received an updated survey form. Compile the results periodically so you will be able to provide prospects with an overview of your skills as a problem solver.

To verify the validity of the survey results, show your customer the self-addressed, stamped envelopes that are directed to the attention of your company's sales manager (marketing director or president), and let him or her know that the surveys are mailed to each customer on a regular basis (every sixty or ninety days).

BE THE AUTHORITY

Because consultative selling is so effective, I recommend that you learn as much as there is to know about your product or service. Learn about your customer's industry as well. The consultant would not have sold his services to the president of the security guard business if he lacked the knowledge or resources that he had developed. Product knowledge means money. The more you know about your product or service, the more solutions you will be able to offer *and* the more sales you will make.

Think of yourself as a problem solver. An engineer has a problem: He needs a sixty-candlepower lightbulb for his newly designed flashlight. The consultative sales professional has the solution. He may suggest a less expensive bulb with a different reflector that will give the engineer the same illumination while increasing the life of the battery because the filament is smaller. As the sales authority in this instance, you probably would enjoy the engineer's business and trust for a long time. Not many salespeople could compete with that kind of product knowledge.

Sales professionals will not always have solutions readily available, but they certainly can tap the knowledge of their engineers and seek assistance in resolving customers' problems.

ORCHESTRATE A SOLUTION

A consultative seller is not unlike an orchestra conductor whose orchestration gives the audience a beautifully coordinated and enjoyable listening experience. Armed with your product knowledge, you orchestrate your management and support personnel in concert to give your customers the kind of consulting know-how they need to meet their goals and objectives.

Just because someone calls himself a salesperson doesn't mean he is a sales consultant. An order taker accepts orders from people who know what they want. A facilitator is an order taker who can help a customer decide which of several similar products she should order. A salesperson introduces his company's products and services in a professional manner, responds positively to objections, and, in a persuasive manner, influences the buying decision to close the sales. But none of the people in these positions has reached the level of sales consultant.

The consultative sales professional determines what the

customer should buy, in what quantities, and how frequently. Because of the problem-solving nature of the relationship, the consultative salesperson earns a long-lasting,
loyal customer following. Even though the consultative
salesperson is in a position to sell the customer something
he or she doesn't need, the salesperson does not violate the
trust the customer has given him.

Everybody talks about *value-added* selling strategies.
"If you advertise in my magazine, I will let you put our
magazine's endorsement on your product or allow you to
sponsor a golf tournament for our subscribers." Each of
these add-ons is a premium benefit that a magazine space-
advertisement salesperson may offer if the customer will
place an advertisement in her magazine.

Sales professionals sell value-added opportunities every
day of the week. One problem is that no one can intelligently compare prices anymore. What is the real value of
sponsoring a subscriber golf tournament? What is the real
value of a magazine's endorsement? What if that magazine
charges $1,000 more for an advertisement than a compet-
itive magazine that has a greater circulation? Is the golf
tournament worth the cost?

As a consultative salesperson, consider your services
the added value. Help the client with better ad positioning
in the magazine or with copy writing or ad layout. If you
do not have the expertise, compile a list of experts with
whom you work as well as outside consultants whom you
can recommend. As a consultative sales professional, you
help, you orchestrate, and you control.

If you are selling homes, find out as much as you can
about your clients' needs. Are they able to make a down
payment and meet mortgage requirements? Do they have a
house to sell before they can physically move? If there is a
handicapped person in the family, the family may want to
be near a rehabilitation center and possibly prefer a one-
story structure. Where do the owners work? Do they need

to be near a specific church or country club? The number of children probably will dictate the number of bedrooms, the size of the yard, and the proximity to schools. Public transportation and proximity to shopping centers, pharmacies, and other retail stores may be an issue for the elderly. How much will it cost them to duplicate the services they currently use? Authors may be concerned about privacy because they work out of their homes. Cottage-industry home owners will require office areas. Some people prefer a brand-new home so they can select the landscaping, wallpaper, location of the master bedroom, and size of the recreation room, while others could care less. Some folks like big kitchens, while others insist on cathedral ceilings in the living room.

Some people have no concept about fixed loans versus variable loans, or the difference in monthly payments at different interest rates. Should they buy with a standard conventional loan, a Federal Housing Authority (FHA) loan, a land contract, or some other method? What if their credit is less than excellent? Can they put more money down and still enjoy a competitive interest rate?

Many people do not know much about buying real estate. Should the title be in joint tenancy or as tenants in common, or should it be held in a living trust? Who should be responsible for what? If the buyer wants to build, are there building restrictions where he or she wants to build? I could come up with a hundred other questions and potential concerns facing the home buyer. Lots of people show homes. Some facilitate, while some sell. The really successful sales professionals use consultative selling techniques to solve their customers' problems.

If you sell residential real estate, why not draft a questionnaire that asks about many of the basic home-buyer requirements? For many people it is easier to list a credit problem than discuss a credit problem. A sample questionnaire would look like the following example.

SAMPLE QUESTIONNAIRE

Buyer's Name(s) _____

Address _____

City _____ State ____ Zip _____

Telephone (home) _____ (business) _____

Do you have any special circumstances or need of which we should be aware while helping you find your new home in the area you desire at a price you can afford?

_____

_____

Do you currently own a home? _____

Is your current home listed for sale? _____

If not, may we list it for you? _____

Is the purchase of your new home contingent on the sale of

   your current home? _____

How much is your current home worth? _____

How much do you owe on your current home? _____

With what firm is your current mortgage held?_____

_____

Do you have a mortgage-lender preference? _____

_____

What price do you have in mind for your new home?

_____

Do you want a fixed- or variable-rate loan for your new

home? _____

What is your household income? _____

Did you recently file for bankruptcy or do you have a bad

credit rating? _____

Do you prefer a single-story condo, a town house, or a

detached single-family home? (circle one)

Do you have children? _____ How many? _____

What are your children's ages? _____

How many bedrooms do you want? _____

What area(s) do you prefer? _____

Please check off all the items that are applicable to your
specific needs:

___ Hardwood floors   ___ Formal dining room
___ Central air-conditioning   ___ Formal living room
___ Den   ___ Recreational room
___ Security system   ___ Gas appliances
___ Electrical appliances   ___ Swimming pool
___ Laundry room   ___ Spa
___ Automatic sprinkler   ___ Sauna
    system   ___ 220-volt power
___ Two-car garage   ___ Attached garage
___ Built-in appliances   ___ Home-maintenance
                                   service contract

On completion of this survey, you can show the prospect everything you have that comes close to meeting his or her specific needs. If needed, you'll be able to introduce the prospect to credit clearance agencies, mortgage bankers, banks, savings-and-loan associations, the chamber of commerce, churches, schools, rehabilitation centers, and referral agencies, as well as provide a list of utility companies with associated connection fees. Most important, you can offer your best advice based on your expert knowledge and recommend solutions to each prospect's home-buying problems. You can control the outcome of the sale, and your sales commissions should soar to the moon.

Service means everything in a society where companies have forgotten what real service is all about. Rewards beyond your wildest imagination can come to a salesperson who knows and incorporates service into his or her daily routines. I would rather have the income of a consultative sales professional than that of most business executives and professional athletes. Business executives often lose their big-paying jobs, and an athlete's years of earning large salaries are few. A consultative sales professional, however, *always* will earn big money, and rightly so. As consumers, we always will need someone to show us the best way to do something, and we are willing to pay for such a valuable service. Just ask the president of that security guard service.

WORK ASSIGNMENT

On a piece of paper, write the names of three prospective customers you've already called on. Beside each name, list several consultative sales ideas that you can use to close the sale.

15
The Ten Best
Closing Techniques

*"Some of us will do our jobs well and some
will not, but we will all be judged by only one
thing—the result."*

—Vince Lombardi

In medieval Japan, businessmen who wished to seal an agreement would urinate together, crisscrossing their streams of urine. Obviously, times have changed. Today, the symbolic gesture when reaching an agreement is the handshake, a simple gesture to make, but not always an easy point to reach in the game of sales.

THE MOST IMPORTANT SKILL

What does it take to close a sale? Good closing techniques can make up for weak presentations and other sales shortcomings. One of the most productive salespeople with whom I have ever worked could hardly speak English, dressed inappropriately, and had little innate sales ability. But could he close a sale! He placed the product in the prospect's hands, and with great enthusiasm, he pointed out the many benefits of ownership. He intuitively knew when the prospect's interest was peaked and then would place the pen in the prospect's hand along with the filled-out order form. Nine times out of ten, the prospect signed.

Closing is winning. I heartily endorse Vince Lombardi's viewpoints on winning:

> Winning is not a sometime thing; it's an all-time thing. You don't win once in a while, you don't do things right once in a while, you do them right all the time. Winning is habit. Unfortunately, so is losing.

Closing means success and improved self-esteem, meeting goals, and enjoying financial freedom. No other skills will help you win in sales more than the development of good closing skills. You can be an expert in every other facet of selling, but if your closing skills are deficient, your sales still will suffer immeasurably. If all of your other sales skills are lacking, but your closing skills are good, you still should perform well in sales.

Closing the sale is the moment of truth. It is the coming together of two parties for mutual benefit. Although it is the culmination of the sales process, closing is more than a conclusion or a finish, because it is hoped you will continue to work with your new or renewed customer for a long time to come. You developed a sales strategy, prospected, followed leads, presented your proposal, addressed every objection, and now Graduation Day is here! You proudly pick up the purchase order, knowing that if it had not been for you, your company would not have the order. Because you did it right, you got the order. Because you developed a good relationship with your customer, you will continue to get the orders. You are great at what you do and your boss knows it, your customer knows it, and, most important, you know it.

WHAT MAKES THE PROSPECT BUY?

People frequently go to great lengths to close a sale. Some churches post the amount of each parishioner's donation on the bulletin board for all to see. Pretty strong closing technique, if you ask me. Many advertising agencies would have you believe that if you do not use their clients' products you will smell bad, look bad, feel bad, or break out in hives. These, too, are pretty strong closing techniques.

Closing techniques will vary depending on the prospect's needs at the time. If your prospect is hungry, it may be pretty easy to sell him or her a sandwich. If he or she has just finished eating, the idea of buying a sandwich might be pretty unappealing. All good things come to those who wait. Sooner or later, the prospect is going to be hungry again, and if you do your job correctly, you will most likely close the sale. You might want to call on your prospect just before the lunch hour. Your super-deluxe turkey sandwich may have less cholesterol, less fat, less sodium and/or fewer calories than any other sandwich. If 22 percent of the population is watching what they eat, it is likely that you will attract 22 percent of the total audience with that one closing technique.

Perhaps you deliver your sandwiches. Many people order food from Domino's Pizza because Domino's delivers in thirty minutes or less or you receive a discount on the pizza. Many pizza parlors have gone out of business because they could not compete with the Domino's Pizza on the corner. Domino's success is testimony that this chain knows how to close. Give the customer fast delivery of a good, quality pizza at competitive prices and, like magic, the sale is closed.

Closing is providing *what* the *prospect* wants *when* the prospect wants it at a *price* that he or she can afford. Sometimes the prospect does not realize that he needs your product or service. Why would someone living in downtown Manhattan want to buy an electricity-generating windmill that's ten stories high? Perhaps because a bright salesperson showed that person a way to use his tax dollars to own an asset. Did the prospect want or need a windmill? Not until he found out about the favorable tax laws and the passive income possibilities. Once the prospect understood the benefits of ownership, he could not buy a windmill fast enough.

Why should a hospital administrator select a guard service from a company other than Pinkerton's, Burns, or any number of major, well-known security guard companies? Because one security guard company specializes in hospital security. The company may charge more, but it renders a service with which no one can compete, so closing a sale becomes relatively easy.

A salesperson selling water-purification filters demonstrates the product by filling a glass of water from the tap and then adding a chemical that makes the chlorine and bacteria visible. This salesperson is likely to close the sale when she attaches a water filter and the chlorine and bacteria disappear. This demonstration puts the prospect in a situation where he realizes, in the presence of the person who can solve the problem, that it would be unconscionable to allow anyone, especially children, to drink such impure, filthy, unfiltered water. What do you think the prospect is going to do?

THE TOP TEN CLOSING TECHNIQUES

On the following pages, I have listed the ten most effective closing techniques. Although there probably are hundreds of types of closes, if you master these ten, you will have an arsenal of closing techniques that will be appropriate for almost any sales situation.

Closing Technique Number One: the Concession Close

The concession close is a very effective technique because it gives your prospect the feeling that you are offering him or her a special deal. Everyone enjoys a bargain. "Buy the car today and I will throw in the extended warranty." "Rent a fishing boat for all day and I will provide you with the bait." Tie the special offer to a fast decision. For example, you might say, "This offer is good for only one week."

Closing Technique Number Two: the Alternative Close

According to an old sales adage, if you can get someone to say "yes" three times, you have a guaranteed sale. If you are a retail salesperson and you ask your potential customer whether he or she wants to use a Visa or Master-Card, whether he or she wants delivery on Monday or Tuesday, and finally, whether he or she wants the item gift wrapped or in a standard box, and each time you get a positive response, the sale is nearly certain. Offer choices that require commitment and phrase the question so that "no" is not an option.

Closing Technique Number Three: the Urgency Close

You probably have heard the urgency close many times. "Buy today because our prices are going up tomorrow!" "We are running out of inventory, so buy now!" "If you do not buy automobile insurance today, it may be too late to buy it tomorrow." "Crime is up in your neighborhood so don't be the next victim! Buy our burglar alarm now." Occasionally, some of these conditions may be exaggerated on the part of the salesperson, but there always are elements of truth in all of them.

It is a lot easier to sell an umbrella when it is pouring rain. Create the sense of urgency when the sun is shining by using word pictures and creating vivid pictures in your prospect's mind. "Imagine walking to work and having your new suit drenched. The bus is always thirty minutes late when you do not have your umbrella. Have you ever noticed how hard it is to buy an umbrella during a downpour?"

Surely your prices will go up from time to time, so give your customers the opportunity to buy *before* prices increase. Your customers will appreciate the lower prices, and you will appreciate the increased business.

Closing Technique Number Four: the Direct Close

Ask for the order. If you have determined a need and the prospect is qualified, simply ask for the order. "With your approval, I would like to start your service at midnight tonight," or "Approve this agreement and I will leave my water softener with you today." Because everyone gets nervous when asked to sign contracts, refer to contracts as agreements, and ask for approval or authorization to ship rather than for a signature.

Sometimes the best combination closing technique is simply to *assume* (assumptive close) the order by filling out your order blank in front of the customer. Then ask for his or her authorization to ship your product (direct close). Pretty easy, huh?

Closing Technique Number Five: the Puppy-Dog Close

Allow your prospect to use the product or service for a few days with the understanding that you'll pick up your product or stop providing the service if he or she doesn't buy. The concept is, of course, that this prospect is going to fall in love with your product or service and decide to pay for it rather than give it back or give it up.

The puppy-dog close is a great closing technique for products that make a prospect's burdens easier to manage. For example, if you allow a janitorial service to use a vacuum cleaner that works better than the one it owns—one that requires less physical exertion—the janitorial service probably will find it difficult to give it back to you. Make the prospect fall in love with your product or service, then use the puppy-dog close: Buy it or give it back. Warning: This closing technique is not recommended for use on people with violent personalities.

Closing Technique Number Six: the Fear-Factor Close

"If you do not buy my water purifier, you will die from bacteria or zinc poisoning or God knows what." "If you don't buy life insurance and you die in a plane crash tomorrow, your wife will be left penniless." One salesperson in San Francisco sold thousands of survival kits to fearful San Francisco residents after the 1989 earthquake.

The fear-factor close is very powerful because you play on people's insecurities, uncertainties, and fears. Everyone wants money in the bank when financial reverses occur. Everyone wants adequate insurance when medical trauma happens. Everyone wants products and services that minimize risks and increase the chances to survive and prosper. If the fear-factor close fits what you are selling, use it.

Closing Technique Number Seven: the Assumptive Close

Simply say to yourself that the prospect has already bought your product. If you do, you will be saying things like, "I wish I could be there when your friends see you driving this great car." "When you trade our car in, you will be very pleased with the high resale value." The prospect will respond as if he or she already owns the car. Write up the order in advance and presume the sale. This is a very powerful closing technique, particularly for reluctant or indecisive customers. Try it on your next prospect, perhaps in conjunction with the direct close.

Closing Technique Number Eight: the Qualifying Close

Each of us is constantly proving ourselves from the cradle to the grave. Did I qualify for awards in scouting? Did I qualify for the cheerleaders' squad in school? Did I qualify to join the armed forces of my choice? Did I qualify to attend the university of my choice? Did I qualify to marry the person of my dreams? Did I qualify to get the home loan I wanted? Each of us wants to qualify, to measure up, to have a sense of acceptance and belonging.

Noted psychologist Abraham Maslow developed a theory of motivation that he described in terms of a hierarchy of needs. Generally, the theory states that once such lower-level needs of food, drink, sex, sleep, safety, belongingness, and love are met, an individual will become motivated by the higher-level needs of *esteem* and *self-actualization*. When you use the qualifying close, you are appealing to a basic human need. You might hear the country-club salesperson say, "We normally require two endorsements by members of our club. However, if you meet our other requirements, because you're new to our city we may be able to waive the endorsement requirement for you." At that point, the prospect does everything in his or her power to meet the other requirements. Sometimes the more difficult you make it to participate, the more value the membership or organization will have, and the harder the prospect will work to qualify. The qualifying close is most effective with prospects who have large egos and who cannot stand rejection.

Closing Technique Number Nine:
the Physical-Action Close

This closing technique demands that you punch the prospect in the face until he or she buys your product. No, just kidding! In this closing technique, you get your prospect physically involved in the sales process. Ask your prospect to help you get the copy machine out of your car. Ask him or her to help you set it up, preferably on the prospect's desk. Walk the prospect through the process of loading the paper, adding toner, running and collating copies. Invite his or her subordinates in and have the prospect demonstrate the machine and all its attributes. During the process, he or she will likely sell himself or herself. This close works because people like to get involved and be a part of the process. Let them.

Closing Technique Number Ten: the Callback Close

Most books you read on sales will discourage callbacks. Strike while the iron is hot and don't give the prospect the opportunity to change his or her mind. If you fail to close the sale on the first sales call, the prospect may receive negative feedback from a spouse, employer, friends, or professional adviser. All of these comments may or may not contain a great deal of truth, but they *will* influence your prospect. As mentioned earlier, the average business-to-business sales call costs $239 today and is predicted to rise to $400 during the 1990s. If you are selling a $500 vacuum cleaner and it takes two sales calls to close the sale, you've just reduced your margin substantially, and you will have lost money when you account for the cost of the vacuum cleaner.

Everyone recognizes, however, that sometimes it simply is not possible to close the sale on the first call. What can you do when a husband or wife states most emphatically that he or she cannot and will not buy anything without his or her spouse's approval? You ask for a signature to hold the price or guarantee product availability for three days. If your prospect gets his or her spouse's approval, you will turn the order in. If not, you will throw away the order. Yes, the prospect has a way out. Under the Federal Trade Commission's three-day cooling off rule, he or she has three business days to cancel certain kinds of contracts anyway, so you really have not given up anything. You simply "conspire" with him or her to overcome the spouse's resistance. Usually when someone signs an agreement, he or she feels obligated to follow through. It's a matter of honor.

When a purchasing agent must obtain the engineering department's approval, ask the purchasing agent to invite the engineer into his or her office and attempt to sell the engineer while you are there. If that is not possible, ask that the purchase order be subject only to the approval of the engineering department within three or five days. Get the commitment in writing, and you will be much closer to consummating a sale.

There is no law that states that you must use one and only one closing technique in any sales situation. You may elect to use all ten closing techniques on the same prospect. I guarantee that one or more is applicable to almost every sales effort.

WHEN DO YOU START TO CLOSE?

You start to close from the time you first meet your prospect until the time you leave. Each effort to close is an attempt at a touchdown. Just because you get tackled as you drive that ball to the end zone does not mean that you walk off the playing field. It's all part of the game, so get up, dust yourself off, develop a new strategy, and make another play. Keep closing until you make the sale.

When closing any sale, it's important to make the prospect commit or tell you what it will take to make him or her commit. Approach the problem of closing intuitively and logically by observing, analyzing, and probing with an open mind.

BE INFLUENTIAL, NOT MANIPULATIVE

Some might argue that these concepts and closing techniques are manipulative. If a physician persuades a patient to undergo a surgical procedure that could save the patient's life, one could say that the physician's manipulation was in the patient's best interest. If a salesperson persuades someone to buy a product that is far superior to the competitors' products and sells it for less money, one could similarly say that his or her manipulation was in the customer's best interest. Manipulating someone for devious, cynical, and unethical reasons is not acceptable. If you influence someone for reasons you consider good, moral, and honorable, you persuade them to do whatever it is that you think will be in his or her own best interest.

Find out what your customer's problems are and persuade him or her to let you solve them. Be so good at influencing your customer that your competitor doesn't stand a chance of getting your customer's business. Remember that a salesperson is measured by the sacrifices he or she is willing to make for the good of the customer in addition to the number of times the salesperson closes sales for the company.

WHAT IF YOU FAIL?

No salesperson will win every sale. Sometimes you will lose—whether it's "the big sale" or a small sale—regardless of how prepared you are to win. In ancient China, doctors were paid when their patients were kept well, not when they were sick. Believing that it was the doctor's job to prevent disease, Chinese doctors often *paid the patient* if the patients became ill. If a patient died, a special lantern was hung outside the doctor's house. With each death, another lantern was hung. As you would expect, too many of these special lanterns resulted in fewer customers.

We all have reminders of our failures. Look at it as Henry Ford did: "Failure is the opportunity to begin again more intelligently." Unfortunately, it generally is mankind's nature to learn from his or her mistakes, not by example. If that's the case, then use your "death lanterns" to light your way to bigger and better things. Knowing how to close the sale will help ensure that the lanterns will surround a palatial estate where a Rolls Royce is parked between an Olympic-sized swimming pool and a tennis court!

16
Five'll Get You Ten

*"On his first day out as a new salesman he
received two orders: 'Get out' and 'Stay out.' "*

—Unknown

I've now covered the five basic personality types and the
ten best closing techniques, but is one closing technique
more effective on a given personality type than another? In
the last chapter, I recommended that, if necessary, you use
all of the closing techniques to close the sale. As a practical
matter, however, your prospect may not give you that
much time. It is far more effective to use the closing techniques that are most appropriate for each of the personality types.

Closing Technique	Personality Types That Respond Best
Concession	Friendly
	—Analytical
	—Situational
Alternative	Persuasive
Urgency......................................	Assertive
	—Situational

Direct .... Assertive
                                               —Analytical
Puppy dog .... Friendly
Fear factor .... Friendly
                                               —Analytical
                                               —Assertive
                                               —Persuasive
                                               —Situational
Assumptive .... Friendly
Qualifying................................... Assertive
                                               —Persuasive
                                               —Situational
Physical action.............................. Assertive
Callback .... Friendly
                                               —Situational

CONCESSION CLOSE

The Friendly personality interprets your concessions as a symbol of your friendship. The Analytical and Situational personalities add your concession offer to the list of reasons why they should buy from you. When your offer includes more positive reasons than negative reasons to buy, you make a sale. It never is a good idea to lead with your best offer. Instead, leave some room to negotiate. The Analytical personality truly enjoys the process of negotiating a good deal, so come in relatively high and let him or her have fun. Even if you give him or her 20 percent off, the negotiated price probably will still be 10 percent more than the price you really wanted in the first place.

ALTERNATIVE CLOSE

The Persuasive personality enjoys interaction and the opportunity to discuss options when you use the alternative closing technique. Each question you ask requires an answer from your prospect and allows him or her to weigh the information before determining the appropriate responses.

URGENCY CLOSE

The Assertive and the Situational personalities react most favorably to the urgency close because it appeals to their task-oriented personalities. "I have a problem, and I want to take care of it now" is what is running through an Assertive personality's brain. The Situational personality reacts similarly but with less intensity to the urgency close. Identify the problem, offer the solution, and use the urgency close.

DIRECT CLOSE

Both the Assertive personality and the Analytical personality respond favorably to the direct close. The Assertive personality is decisive and always is busy doing three things at once, so he or she wants to get to the bottom line. Give Assertive personalities the facts and the chance to order now with immediate delivery, and they usually will buy. The Analytical personality reacts positively to the direct close because it places him or her in a position to make an informed decision early in the sales process. The Analytical personality knows time is money and believes salespeople tend to talk too much, and consequently would just as soon get the facts, make a decision, and get back to work.

PUPPY-DOG CLOSE

Why does the Friendly personality readily accept the puppy-dog close? Allowing the prospect to test your product or service for a few days means that you trust him or her. A solid friendship is based on trust and mutual respect, and your prospect won't want to let you down by returning your product after you've been so kind.

FEAR-FACTOR CLOSE

Every personality type responds to the fear-factor close. It is so powerful because of its universality. If you are getting mixed signals from a prospect and aren't sure which closing technique to employ, consider the fear-factor close.

Most people react in the same way when a revolver is pointed at them: They become afraid. Most people respond similarly when they believe that their lifestyle, health, financial security, or the safety of loved ones is in jeopardy. Sometimes the *fear* of being vulnerable is as strong and pervasive as actually being vulnerable.

At one point in my career, I was given the responsibility of managing large quantities of precious metals. I would lay awake at night imagining what it would be like to be held up by an armed robber who demanded the thousands of ounces of gold, silver, and platinum in my charge. I heard stories of managers in other parts of the world who were bound and gagged and forced to listen to the thieves discussing whether or not to shoot the witnesses. So it was easy for the burglar-alarm salesperson to sell me motion detectors and window, door, floor, and ceiling alarms. I even hired an armed guard. It was only after I heard about the terror suffered by my fellow managers that I wanted to purchase every conceivable mode of protection. Do not assume that your prospect fully understands what can happen if he or she fails to buy products or services that would ensure a certain style of living, continued good health, financial security, or personal safety.

If you are selling hospitalization insurance, show your prospects what could happen to them without hospitalization coverage. Picturing yourself in a ward of a county hospital receiving less than adequate health care is not a comforting thought. In addition, on your release, the county legally could attach your belongings to pay the bill. The salesperson can tell the prospect that he or she can avoid that horror by purchasing hospitalization insurance.

No matter what you are selling, there is an appropriate fear-factor close. A purchasing agent could cause a factory's production line to stall if a critical component is faulty, or if delivery is delayed. Imagine how a purchasing agent would feel knowing that his or her actions were holding up production for a day or even a week. The consequences would be unthinkable.

ASSUMPTIVE CLOSE

The Friendly personality appreciates the assumptive close because it connotes acceptance and allows this person to remove himself or herself from the difficult task of saying "no." Friendly personalities are typically nonconfrontational. Rejecting a salesperson, a salesperson's products, or a sales premise is a confrontational act, an act that is out of character for the Friendly type. Unconsciously, Friendly personalities will assume that they led you to believe they wanted to buy, and they won't want to hurt your feelings. The assumptive close coupled with the concession close is a lethal combination where the Friendly personality is concerned. Write up the order, make concessions as you go along, and the Friendly prospect will almost certainly buy.

QUALIFYING CLOSE

The Assertive personality, the Persuasive personality, and the Situational personality find the qualifying close difficult to ignore. The Assertive personality tends to be a bit insecure and wants to belong yet has difficulty with things that take time. He or she wants to belong and wants to belong *now*. Give him or her the ability to join or buy now and you have made a sale. The Situational personality generally reacts the same way.

The Persuasive personality seeks to identify with groups of people and products that reflect favorably on him or her. Both Assertive and Persuasive personalities tend to buy prestigious automobiles and live in large homes in more affluent neighborhoods. Material assets make a statement for them, and they enjoy belonging to any special group if they qualify. Sell more than you have ever sold before by helping the Assertive, Persuasive, or Situational prospect qualify with good financing plans, good support services, leasing programs, and alternative choices.

PHYSICAL-ACTION CLOSE

The Assertive personality is so busy that she barely finds time to eat. The Assertive personality's overactive mind moves from idea to idea. She talks to you while answering the telephone or writing letters. Use the physical-action close on the Assertive personality as it will force her to pay attention and get involved. If the Assertive personality is thoroughly involved in the sales process, she will sell herself as well as everybody else.

CALLBACK CLOSE

The Friendly personality and the Situational personality relate to the callback close because it means a return visit from you, which they intuitively like because of the good relationship that has developed between the two of you. This closing technique relieves the pressure of needing an immediate decision made during your initial call. A call-back provides the Friendly personality with a comfort zone, but it also gives you a *tentative* commitment. Attempt to use the concession close, the puppy-dog close, the fear-factor close, or the assumptive close before the callback close because it's always better to get the order without any conditions or contingencies while you are there.

WHICH CLOSES WORK BEST WITH THE SITUATIONAL PERSONALITY?

Although someone with a Situational personality could respond favorably to *all* of the closing techniques, he or she will respond positively with the most intensity to the concession close, the urgency close, the fear-factor close, the qualifying close, and the callback close. By trying these closing techniques, you'll be selling to those personality characteristics in greatest preponderance in this particular personality type.

THE POWER TO WIN

Success in sales is more a matter of concentration, perseverance, and hard work than it is of raw talent or opportunity. Winners make the most of their minds and bodies by identifying their attributes, abilities, and skills, and applying them where they would do the most good. Winners do not ask for tasks equal to their talents; they ask for powers equal to their tasks. These closing strategies, coupled with personality-assessment techniques, will empower you with the ability to close every qualified prospect you encounter. Combine this power with hard work and perseverance, and you, too, will become one of the world's best salespeople.

17
Who's Maintaining
Market Share?

*"Old salespeople never die—they just get out of
commission."*

—Unknown

If you are the greatest sales professional in the world and
you are closing each and every prospect, you are truly one
in a million. If you are *keeping* each and every customer
after making the initial sale, and you are able to sell re-
peatedly to the same customer every time, you are one in a
trillion (and should be writing your *own* sales book).

Most sales professionals probably close one out of five
qualified prospects, depending on the type of product or
service and whether or not they are selling a proprietary
product or service. Before the U.S. Post Office, UPS, and
Airborne began their overnight delivery programs, Federal
Express was the only reasonably priced method available
to ship packages overnight. Because Federal Express initi-
ated the first U.S. overnight delivery service on a routine
basis and invented the hub-and-spokes distribution system, I suspect that the Federal Express sales representative had a pretty easy sales job on his or her hands. As the

competition came on board, it probably became increasingly more difficult to close new clients and keep old clients. As the marketplace became more competitive, customers had more options and could compare the advantages and disadvantages of each overnight delivery service.

If you are fortunate enough to sell a proprietary product or service, qualified prospects are compelled to buy from you or go without the product or service that you are selling. Before the divestiture of Ma Bell, Bell Telephone was not compelled to hire the best sales talent in the world because there was no competition. Today, with thousands of well-trained, seasoned professionals from private telephone companies offering a host of communication miracles, that certainly is not the case. The Bell salesperson probably had a pretty difficult time making the transition from his or her previous role to that of a proactive, aggressive seller in a highly competitive marketplace.

You may never have had the pleasure of selling a proprietary product. Perhaps you always have sold more common, "me, too," kinds of things, such as barbecue sets, automobiles, cereal, or pencils. Before you concede that your product is pretty much the same as your competitors', find out what your customers think. You may be pleasantly surprised. They may have established a brand loyalty or decided that some other feature or benefit (such as country of origin or colors available) is weighted heavily in their buying decisions. Packaging may be the critical factor in their choice. Are they one of the 20 percent whose decisions are purely price driven? Don't make assumptions.

MAKE IT EXCITING

No matter how exciting (or boring, if that's the case) your product or service may be, no matter how many competitors you have, you must make your company, your products, and your presentation exciting. If all other things are equal—price, availability, size, color, packaging, financing, and warranty—why should your prospects buy their initial supply or future supply requirements from you?

MAKE YOURSELF VISIBLE

Let's assume that whatever you did the first time worked, and that your prospect actually purchased one full year's worth of pencils from you. Perhaps you used the concession close and gave your customer a free pencil for every twenty he purchased. Perhaps you allowed your customer to buy this year's supply of your product at the past year's prices. Today, while examining the computerized sales sheets at the office, you notice that your customer has not bought any pencils for five weeks. You immediately call him and hurriedly ask his secretary to ring you through.

Your customer tells you that he recently switched to another supplier because the new supplier will provide pencils in the corporation's colors for no additional charge. When you ask him if he knew that your company could provide the same products, he tells you that he may have known that at one time but simply forgot it because you had not come by to see him in almost a year. Before terminating the call, he says somewhat matter-of-factly that you really should call on your customers more often.

Maintaining market share can be extraordinarily tough. Closing one out of five prospects while losing three out of five existing customers may be the quickest road to the professional junkyard. It's certainly not the route to the front of the sales commission pay line.

ONCE I'VE GOT IT, HOW DO I KEEP IT?

Let's assume that you have mastered the sales techniques, strategies, and guidelines, and you are closing most of your prospects. Welcome to the One-in-a-Million Sales Professional Club of America! Now you are faced with the other major sales problem: *How do I keep the business?*

The first rule in successfully maintaining your customer base is to be visible and available. Don't give your customer the impression that now that she's given you her business you've abandoned her. Let your existing customers know just how important they are on a regular basis. Periodically check in with them by telephone. When a new product is introduced, send them an advance notice. If prices are going up or special discounts become available, let them know so they can take advantage of the information.

A good personal computer and printer is your first line of defense. (See Appendix B, "What Sales and Marketing Software Are the Professionals Using?".) You need a software program(s) with a tickler file, calendar, card index, and call-reporting and word-processing features. Then you need a cartoon caricature of you on a pair of skis sliding down a mountain out of control and one of you lying on a beach.

Yes, two caricatures. When you go on vacation, send a copy of one of the caricatures to all of your customers with a note saying that you are going on vacation, when you are leaving, and when you intend to return. Also, tell your customers who they can reach at your company if they need products or service while you are out of the office. Your sense of humor and concern for their welfare in your absence will be appreciated and *remembered.*

Your personal computer should be used to maintain your customer card index and call reports. Your tickler file should be programmed to advise you at least sixty days before a customer contract is scheduled to elapse. Check your tickler file each morning. As a customer name appears, set up appointments and make courtesy calls so that you will have enough time to counter any internal or external obstacles to effectuating renewal. This process is extremely important for media sales representatives where multiple advertisement orders are concerned.

Use the tickler file to remind you of customers' birthdays, anniversaries, and other important dates. Send greeting cards, short notes, or small gifts to let your customers know that you care about them personally. The gifts should be symbols of your appreciation of them as your customers, such as framed certificates of appreciation, paperweights, or inexpensive, unique gifts. Never send expensive gifts. You certainly wouldn't want to inadvertently break your customer's corporate policy or have him or her accused of accepting bribes.

Offer training and advice to customers. If they come to rely on this, they'll probably keep buying from you. Make your company, your products, and yourself indispensable, and your competitor never will get in the front door.

Use your computer to produce a one- or two-page newsletter for your customers. I met one insurance salesman in Nebraska who publishes a one-page newsletter to provide his clients with the steady stream of information that they need. His newsletter answers questions such as: Can a client borrow on her term life insurance policy or on her whole life insurance policy? After someone dies, are the insurance proceeds taxable? In a divorce, do insurance cash values have to be divided in a community-property state? This salesman also receives permission to reprint the many interesting facts that he finds in industry trade newsletters.

Then he uses the newsletter to advertise new insurance programs and benefits. And he highlights actual case studies of clients who've been seriously ill or who've been victims of fire, home burglaries, or automobile theft to illustrate how the insurance company expediently handled the victims' problems in a sensitive, caring fashion.

This same salesperson also decided to form a softball team in his community and used the newsletter to recruit team members. Although he covered the team's triumphs and losses, he also had the opportunity to feature his clients in his write-ups of the ball games. His clients had fun while actively participating in the salesperson's continued success.

Start a newsletter and your customers will respect the fact that you think enough of them to provide them with up-to-date information about your product or service, the latest industry news, and other information that directly affects their lives. The high visibility will keep you in the minds of your customers and demonstrate your professionalism.

DO YOU REALLY KNOW WHAT
YOUR CUSTOMER THINKS?

Consider using focus groups to discuss your customers' experiences with your product, suggest possible changes for the next generation of your product or service, or help solve a particular industry problem. The focus groups can be made up of customers *or* potential customers. Keep the two groups separate and compare the results. Arrange a luncheon in each of the geographical areas within your territory, and invite your designated focus group members to discuss your product over lunch (which you are providing, of course).

During lunch, invite your existing customer group members to tell each other how they are using your products. Control the focus group meeting by preparing an agenda and adhering to it. Your job is to keep the meeting moving, informative, light, and interesting. One customer may give another customer an idea about your product or service that will result in increased sales and stronger support for you and your product. You are the beneficiary of concrete feedback about your product in addition to the enhanced goodwill you have created. And, the meeting is a great networking opportunity for all concerned.

When I was publishing a magazine for heart-disease patients, I formed focus groups that met monthly. I asked the fifteen nurses at my first focus meeting if they were recommending my magazine to the heart patients in their cardiac rehabilitation units. All but one said "yes." The one nurse who did not respond affirmatively said that she gave the magazine to *every patient over forty* who was discharged from the hospital because everyone over forty was at risk. Moreover, she wished that all of her patients would read the magazine because everyone should live the heart-healthy lifestyle the magazine espoused.

As a result of her comments and the discussions of other focus groups, my sales doubled over the period of one year. As an added bonus, my customers were regularly reminded that I cared about their opinions, their hospitals, and their patients.

Do you care about your customers? Have their needs changed recently? What do they think would make your product or service better? Are you in touch with your customers on a regular basis? How often do they need to see you? Are you truly interested in what they think? No matter what your field, if you care about your customers' well-being and want to maintain your market share, form focus groups. I do not care whether you form groups of farmers talking about your fertilizer, stockbrokers talking about investments, or racehorse owners talking about your rent-a-jockey service. You always can benefit from listening to your customers.

Be creative in terms of the benefits of contract or purchase-order renewals. It always amazes me how a salesperson won't hesitate to spend inordinate amounts of money on sales calls, lunches, and dinners to secure a *new* account. He or she uses every closing technique under the sun to get the business initially. But when it comes time for a customer to renew the business, the salesperson is nowhere in sight.

Perhaps you could arrange for the delivery of doughnuts to your customer's office each morning for a week on the anniversary of the customer's contract renewal. We've all heard the old saying, "It's the thought that counts." Well, this is one time when what you give really isn't so important as finding a way to remember the customer and let him or her know you appreciate his or her business.

When I was an integrated-circuit salesperson, I gave a special gift to every customer on his contract renewal date: encapsulated integrated circuits mounted on silver-plated cuff links. Because no one could buy a pair, these unusual cuff links were the envy of a multitude of electronics contractors' purchasing agents. The only way to obtain a pair was to become a repeat customer of mine.

Remember the Golden Rule? I can think of no better advice on how to treat your customers. Take good care of your customers and they will take good care of you. You worked so hard to get them; are you ready to give them up so easily? Disappoint them or ignore them, and they most certainly will disappoint you. Remember: If you don't let your customer know how important he or she is, one of your competitors surely will.

18
What Men Don't Tell
Women in Sales

*"People's minds are changed through
observation, and not through argument."*

—Will Rogers

While much lip service has been given to equal opportunity in the workplace, I do not see any great progress being
made. Women still work at a decided disadvantage in the
business world and continue to be judged more harshly
than men in certain fields. Although the gender gap reportedly is narrowing, corporate chief executive officer meetings throughout the United States still are dominated by
males, and many companies still predominantly hire men
to sell for them.

If sales managers think that the job of selling should be
reserved only for the tough, modern-day male gladiators,
they should think again. Many qualified women are quite
capable of closing the big sales with their professional
sales skills. (Besides, you are not supposed to throw your
prospects to the lions!) Do men scheme against women,
sabotage their work efforts, betray them, backbite, envy
their success, and get jealous if women outsell them? Yes,

but perhaps not any more than men might do to each other.

According to the Families and Work Institute, approximately two-thirds of the people entering the work force today are women. I probably don't have to tell you that, to some extent, a woman still may find herself a victim of the traditional view of a woman's role in a society where business has been dominated by men. The U.S. Bureau of Labor Statistics figures show that working women still earn 30 percent less than men on the average, although the percentage varies by the specific industry. A report by Catalyst, a research organization for women in corporations, reveals that of the 35.6 million women who currently work full-time, 98 percent earn less than $50,000 annually. Only 0.3 percent of women working full-time earn more than $78,000 annually, although approximately eight times as many men earn that amount.

SALES IS ONE OF THE BEST CAREER CHOICES

The purpose of this chapter is not to expose the underlying fallacies that have been used to keep women in subservient positions in business in the past but to rethink what it means to be a woman—specifically a saleswoman—in today's workplace. While women may encounter glass ceilings or find it impossible to enjoy the benefits of some of the Good Old Boys' Clubs, many women are finding that they have an excellent opportunity to make a significant six-figure income in a sales career. Business writer Sarah Stiansen Mahoney evaluated the best jobs for women to pursue in the coming millennium in the July/August 1991 *Executive Female*. Traditional sales and network marketing sales (direct sales) were two of the ten fields noted. In the same article, Dan Lacey, editor of *Workplace Trends* newsletter, states that the ability to sell will be the most important skill needed to succeed in business in the future.

In many respects, females have distinct advantages over males in the sales arena. In a sales setting, women often are considered more approachable than men. Although some saleswomen use aggressiveness very effectively, salesmen generally tend to be more aggressive on the whole. Saleswomen often tend to be more empathetic than salesmen, and they successfully use their empathy to respond to customer objections and to sell the benefits of the product. These "humanizing" techniques help reduce a customer's stress level in a sales meeting. Many sales professionals believe that people generally feel more comfortable with women salespeople. Additionally, many women in sales are detail oriented and excel in handling the planning aspects of selling, which makes them thorough and long range in their thinking.

Many businesspeople have remarked that women in business tend to be more honest than men, which could make them more trustworthy in a prospect's eyes. Mary Kay Ash, founder and chairperson of Mary Kay Cosmetics, sought to create a business atmosphere in which a woman's special sensitivities and talents could be encouraged, not discouraged. Her corporate philosophy is to operate according to the principle of the Golden Rule, a belief that many did not see having a place in the traditional, competitive business world. Yet, Mary Kay Cosmetics has been extraordinarily successful.

Historically, many saleswomen have had problems handling the rejection that is so much a part of sales. Deborah Tannen, Ph.D., professor at Georgetown University, reports in *Executive Female* (January/February 1991) that many women lack experience in defending themselves (or their products, in this case), and they may misinterpret objections as representing personal attacks on their credibility. According to Professor Tannen, women speak and hear a language related to personal feelings of intimacy, connection, and being liked, while the language of men is geared toward gaining respect and independence. Remember: Rejection should not be taken personally, and every salesperson—regardless of sex—wins some and loses some.

Going for the jugular when closing has been difficult for many women in sales, but by mastering the necessary techniques, they can overcome this problem. Anticipating and answering objections is a learnable skill. Generally, the more seasoned a salesperson becomes, the more any differences of assertiveness attributed to gender disappear.

WHAT SHOULD YOU SELL?

Financial planners sometimes employ an investment technique called *contrarian investments*. Simply stated, when the market is falling and everyone else is selling to minimize their losses, you buy. Conversely, as the market is rising and everyone else is buying, you sell. The theory basically implies that all financial markets rise and fall depending on fundamental, technical, and psychological changes perceived by the buying public and financial institutions. The contrarian theory works. The Rockefellers amassed a fortune during the Great Depression. While bankers, stockbrokers, and investors were leaping from tall buildings, the Rockefellers were buying stocks for pennies on the dollar. After the depression, stock prices rose to their predepression value and the Rockefellers sold. Pretty smart folks, those Rockefellers.

Consider the contrarian theory in terms of a career as a saleswoman. My advice to a saleswoman seeking to rise to the top is: Do not work in a business dominated by saleswomen. Instead, consider a career in construction, aircraft, automobile, or computer sales, in military or government sales, or in another industry traditionally controlled by men. The mere fact that you are a woman and are in such an industry will make you highly visible and set you apart from everyone else.

Industrial sales is less than wide open to women and will offer challenges that a male counterpart probably wouldn't have to face. Your customers may question your competence simply because you're a female. You may encounter more sexual prejudices or even sexual harassment in this type of setting, whether it's in the form of jokes or blatantly sexist behavior. First meetings are often awkward, but once you show that you're knowledgeable about your product and highly competent, you should be able to get past the initial testing that may occur. On the other hand, some women in industrial sales often find that they are treated better than their male counterparts.

A woman may need to walk a fine line with prospects; she shouldn't have to hide the fact that she's a woman, yet she won't want to appear coy or manipulative by flaunting her femininity. If you act either too feminine or too masculine, you may find yourself on the outside looking in. Wearing a National Organization for Women (NOW) pin and engaging in male bashing are not suggested behaviors. The goal is to be a successful salesperson in what has traditionally been a male bastion. This will probably require a woman to be a team player, and that may not always be an easy task. That's when empathetic abilities and a good sense of humor may help the most.

BE READY FOR THE TEST: DO YOUR HOMEWORK

Now that you have your prospects' attention, you must exude professionalism if you are going to be the most successful salesperson in the company. Because you're a woman, you'll probably be quizzed or put through your paces by your prospects. To remain graceful under pressure, you must be well prepared in all areas of sales, from probing to closing. You'll especially want to learn *everything* there is to know about your company and its products. Because your products may be highly technical, study them well. Compose a complete list of features and benefits. Read the warranties; ask about financing plans, leasing programs, and trial-offer opportunities. You'll want to know every possible way that your prospect can own your products, so do your homework. Many times, the decision on whether or not to buy is predicated on the availability of financing. Dedicate yourself to being the best by keeping on top of the latest developments in the field.

WHAT KIND OF IMAGE SHOULD YOU PROJECT?

Now that you have selected your career and your market, and you've learned more about your products than even their inventors know, take a good look at your image. What kind of first impression do you make?

As mentioned in Chapter 9, "Power Presentations That Work," the choice of clothing you select depends on many considerations, including your personal taste, your customer, the corporate and industry culture, the occasion, the geography, and your physical appearance. As a woman, you must be particularly sensitive to the image and impression you create. The key to successful dressing for today's woman is to maintain one's individuality. The goal is to be personally distinctive and communicate your self-confidence.

Today, a woman can be professional and still be comfortable with her femininity. First and foremost, you must appear credible and professional. Take your cues from your customer. Your personal "look" should not interfere with the reason you are there—to make a sale. You don't want anything to distract your prospect from the merits of your presentation.

As a general rule, unless you are selling fertilizer to farmers or visiting construction sites, dress professionally in quality, stylish suits, or dresses or tailored pants with *jackets*. A jacket connotes authority. Accent your attire with colorful accessories and simple, classic jewelry. You should not overdress or wear apparel that is revealing, tight, or faddish. Remember: You will be selling to people of all ages, ethnic groups, and religious persuasions. You certainly want to make an impact, but make sure it's a favorable one.

You are a saleswoman who wants to be taken seriously, so your hairstyle also should be a consideration. It should not be too extreme or too elaborate and should not require a lot of maintenance during the day. Getting in and out of cars all day long in the elements can make certain hairstyles difficult to manage. On occasion, you may be required to wear a hard hat, protective ear gear, or other garb that could ruin an elaborate hairstyle for the rest of the day.

DON'T LOSE YOUR SENSE OF HUMOR

According to Dr. Barbara Mackoff, being too serious can keep you from getting ahead. In her book *What Mona Lisa Knew* (Los Angeles: Lowell House), she reports the results of a survey of 200 corporate executives who were asked to name the qualities that keep women from rising to the top of the corporate ranks. Lack of a sense of humor was close to the top of the list.

Humor communicates, conveys authority, builds rapport, defuses conflict, and motivates. Women should avoid playing the court jester and repeating off-color jokes, and self-deprecating humor should be held to a minimum, but, Dr. Mackoff suggests, a woman can effectively use humor in an understated, occasional fashion that allows her unique style and personality to create a powerful presence. Humor is a great stress reliever, so don't leave home without it.

HANDLING AWKWARD SITUATIONS

Because more women are entering the sales force every day, the chance that a woman will encounter a sexual-abuse situation—from customers or associates—is greater than ever before. One person's flirtation may be another's discomfort, and a clearly defined set of rules doesn't exist for every situation. As most women can attest, not all forms of sexual abuse are blatantly physical but may include a broad range of behaviors. Because being sociable often is such a large part of sales, men may misinterpret certain actions or may perceive mixed signals from women. For instance, a colleague or a prospect may read more into the motives behind a saleswoman's luncheon invitation than was intended.

Obviously, the response to improper suggestions or harassment will vary according to the particular situation and the individual involved. Women should be aware that the Equal Employment Opportunity Commission (EEOC) has established guidelines concerning harassment in the workplace, including the need for a written corporate policy prohibiting unlawful harassment. The days of easy dismissals of sexual harassment claims are drawing to a close. If you have any questions concerning your company's policy, check with your manager or your company's Human Resources Department.

Sales & Marketing Management magazine (October 1989) reports that although there are many ways to respond to an outright physical- or verbal-abuse situation, the best strategy is one of prevention. To avoid getting into potentially dangerous situations, *Sales & Marketing Management* cites the following preventive measures:

1. Make sure your behavior is always professional.
2. Wear appropriate business attire.
3. To maintain control, do not drink at business functions.
4. Don't become too friendly.
5. As much as possible, avoid being alone.
6. Make sure you have independent transportation.
7. Make sure your colleagues consider you one of the gang, and accept their support.
8. Join female networking groups for support, encouragement, and reinforcement.
9. Trust your instincts about people.
10. If a situation warrants, ask to be removed from an account.

Although you may be tempted to become involved in the personal lives of your colleagues and customers, insist on an arm's-length business relationship at all times. When you attend sales meetings, conventions, and business dinners, retain your professional demeanor and control the conversation by keeping it focused on the customer. Use your probing skills to find out more about the customer's company or his or her interests. If you are unable to schedule a meeting in your customer's office, meet for breakfast instead of dinner or lunch. Whenever traveling alone, be very aware of your surroundings and more vigilant about your safety.

So what do you do when your customer tries to take control away from you? Evaluate the situation to determine your approach. Is confrontation warranted? Will humor defuse the uncomfortable nature of the moment? Is documentation necessary? Does the situation warrant a physical retreat? If possible, it is always best to avoid humiliating the other party, but use your own judgment regarding the best way to deliver your response.

Should you elect to become involved with a customer on a personal level, you will be courting disaster. This warning also applies to salesmen who might be contemplating such a move. Should your customer's boss or management find out, your customer's professional judgment will be questioned. He or she may be directed to stop doing business with you just to eliminate any question of impropriety. If the relationship does not work out, your customer may cancel your contract just to eliminate those uncomfortable feelings that would surely accompany your return visits. If your customer talks to other customers, this could damage your reputation throughout the industry. Rather than go on with the multitude of problems associated with having a personal relationship with a customer, let me state for the record that it is not a good idea. If you are considering such a move, please reconsider.

Should an uncomfortable comment or situation occur, I believe there always is only one attitude to adopt. It is the same response that I give to a client who asks for a bribe: "I am not going to place myself or you in a compromising position." However you decide to get the message across, let the party know that you don't mix business with your personal life.

Dr. Mackoff suggests that a sense of levity may be the best way to distance yourself from the advances of a customer. For instance, when a customer plants his hand on your thigh, Dr. Mackoff suggests that a humorous response may effectively defuse the situation. "I think your hand is lost" or "What, and destroy both of our fantasies?" probably will establish the proper limits without destroying the professional relationship.

The more professional you are, the more professional your prospects, customers, and colleagues will be. Insist that you be treated with respect, not because you are a woman, but because you have worked hard to be a very competent sales professional. Be selective, however, when choosing your battles. Learn to distinguish between what is and what isn't worth getting upset about.

PUTTING IT ALL TOGETHER

Some of the most successful sales professionals I know are women. Sheila Cluff started her health and fitness business in Ojai, California, out of her home with little cash and a whole lot of sales ability. In 1990, her company billed $7 million in sales.

During a recent meeting with Sheila at her Ojai headquarters, I could not help but notice her warm reception, firm handshake, product knowledge, professional demeanor, sophisticated bearing, attractive suit, stylish but easy-to-manage short hair, great eye contact, and warm personality. After just two minutes with this incredible woman, I realized that she epitomizes the consummate saleswoman. Yes, the $7 million in sales the past year is great, but the quality of this human being is even greater. I immediately trusted her and wanted to do business with her. I intuitively knew that Sheila would not sell me anything that I did not need. If I purchased something from her, I knew that she would make certain that I was pleased with what I bought. Sheila believes in her services, she believes in her company, and from her confidence and professional demeanor, you know that she believes in herself.

Whether you are a man or a woman, as a determined sales professional, you can achieve the loftiest goals by giving professionalism a high priority in everything you do.

19
The Magic of Working for Yourself

"Opportunity does knock occasionally but it is usually just another salesperson."

As I mentioned earlier, the average cost of a business-to-business sales call is $239, reports *Sales & Marketing Management* magazine (January 1990), and predictions are that the average cost will skyrocket to $400 during this decade. In a survey with Personnel Corporation of America, the magazine found that the overall cost of one sale averages 14.5 percent of the total sales volume of a company, but at some businesses it can escalate to as high as 35 percent. This cost includes the salesperson's salary, commissions, benefits, expenses, and administrative support. The survey also reported that to close a first sale requires an average of *seven* calls, while sales with established customers require only three calls.

A WINNING ALTERNATIVE

A great percentage of small to medium-sized companies simply cannot afford to keep salespeople on staff. If they have a product distributed regionally or nationally, their costs go up exponentially in some cases; instead of paying automobile expenses, they are buying airline tickets and paying expensive hotel bills. As an alternative, they could hire additional sales staff in other regions or cities, but they'd have to hire sales managers and worry about whether or not calls are being made. I personally knew one salesman who worked for three companies at the same time. He was actually on three separate payrolls. When he took a customer out to dinner, he submitted the dinner expense to all three companies. All of the companies were in the medical field, but none of them was competing with the others. This type of person—sometimes referred to as "The Salesman from Hell"—is the small business owner's worst nightmare.

Such nightmare types are part of the reason that independent sales representatives are in great demand. They pay their own expenses and make nothing unless they sell something. Using independent representatives, a small company can afford to have representation in every major city in North America and probably throughout the world. If a company pays an independent representative a 20 percent commission, it usually caps its sales expenses below that of its competitors and only pays for *results*. I know independent publishers' representatives who earn more than $1 million a year selling advertising space in magazines. I knew one independent manufacturer's representative in Chicago who made more than $1 million a year selling electronic components.

SELECTING A PRODUCT

If you are in sales now, or believe you have good sales potential, the independent sales representative business may be just right for you. It is very easy to get started. First, decide what product or service you want to sell. Pick something that you can get *passionate* about. If you love bicycling, for example, contact the manufacturer of a bicycle that you think is better than other bicycles in a similar class. Ask the sales manager if the company has representation in your area. Then ask if the manager would be interested in hiring a sales representative on a straight commission basis. If the answer is "yes," you are off and running!

The same call can be made to manufacturers of every product imaginable. Do you want to sell x-ray machines, television sets, pianos, towels, linen service, advertising, television commercials, or airplanes? Each of these products or services has independent representatives selling in the marketplace.

I know one salesperson who sold remodeling services for a construction company. He earned a salary of $4,000 a month and 1 percent commission on sales. His commission brought him an average of $500 a month. That gave him an average monthly paycheck of $4,500 and an annual salary and commission of approximately $54,000. His employer suddenly filed for bankruptcy and the salesperson was out of a job. At the time that he was let go, the salesperson had thirty to forty pending construction jobs ranging in value from $5,000 for a kitchen-cabinet installation job to $170,000 for building a guest house on a millionaire's country estate. The salesperson contacted two of his old competitors for a job. He was anxious to earn a commission on the many pending jobs that he felt confident he could close.

With time passing and his competitors now hot on the trail of these jobs, he contacted a medium-sized construction company on the other side of town, but it could not afford a salesperson; the owner made all of the sales calls. After a brief discussion with the owner, the salesperson struck a deal by which the owner agreed to pay him 20 percent on all the sales he could make. The salesperson sold eleven of the jobs in the first week. He handed $139,000 worth of business to the owner of the construction company and earned $27,800. He went on to earn more than $200,000 in his first year. The salesperson wondered why he did not go into business for himself ten years earlier.

HOW TO GET STARTED

As an independent sales representative, you'll want to open a small office, order your stationery and business cards, and open a bank account. Of course, a personal computer would be a real plus in managing your accounts and your business.

Talk to your attorney about forming a corporation and drafting an agreement between you and the company you want to sell for. He or she can advise you of other legal considerations and the types of insurance you might need. You may wish to contact The Manufacturers' Agents National Association (23016 Mill Creek Road, Laguna Hills, CA 92653, (714) 859-4040) for membership information and a copy of its contractual guidelines booklet.

Your sales representative agreement should state that you are a free agent and not an employee. Define your territory well. In some cases, it may be all of North America; in other cases, it may be a single market segment in one city. You may be able to negotiate reimbursement of your out-of-pocket expenses, but that is very unusual. Make sure that all purchase orders go to you first so that you will be able to keep track of your sales. Your contract probably will provide for payments to you within thirty days after your client (manufacturer) receives payment from your customer. So make sure you have some operating capital to weather any periods of slow cash flow.

One word of caution: It is not uncommon for an independent sales representative to establish a good money-making territory only to receive a representation termination letter, which is just the opposite of what normally happens when you perform well as a salesperson employed by a company. Once you have developed a territory that's really producing, your client's management may decide to stop paying you $50,000 to $200,000 or more and hire its own salesperson for considerably less money. One way to discourage your client from doing this is to include in your original agreement a termination clause that mandates a six-month extension of your contract for each year of service. If you have been selling for your client for five years, he or she owes you a two-and-a-half-year extension. That will make it pretty difficult to let you go.

Eventually, you can hire salespeople to work for you for a draw against commissions and a 10 percent commission. The really big money is made when you start earning one-half the commissions of five, ten, or twenty other sales professionals.

20
The Road Map to Genuine Sales Success

"Success is a journey, not a destination."

—Ben Sweetland

Be certain that a sales career is what you want. It can be nerve racking waiting for purchase orders. Losing a major customer is not fun. Unlike many other occupations, your abilities always are on parade. You can be the number-one sales achiever one year and number 101 the next year. Sales can be a pretty tough job at times. The fact that it is a tough job is precisely why it pays so well if you are good at it.

If you're determined to be a champion in the sales game, how do you find the winner's circle? It is hard to have a successful journey without knowing where you are going or how you are going to get there. You must establish your sales goals and ask yourself where you want to be one year from now. Your answer will dictate how hard and how smart you'll need to work to get there. Establish your goals and head down the road. Ladies and gentlemen, start your engines.

The road map to real success and prosperity in sales is

much the same as it is in other professions. Be integrity based, work hard, use sound judgment, be enthusiastic, and know your product better than anyone else. Practice the basic skills until their execution is second nature. Network, smartly package your sale, use synergistic sales techniques, and employ consultative selling methods. Maintain this course, and you will navigate your way along the sales professional's road map to success.

Your integrity is your vehicle. Your skills are the fuel to get you to your destination. Your determination is the four-lane highway. Your sense of humor will make the trip easier and more enjoyable. There is room in your vehicle for family, friends, and loved ones. If you take it slow and steady and possess the required amount of self-confidence, you will make it. There will be a few other great salespeople making the journey alongside you: other successful salespeople who also learned the magic formula to sales success.

An issue often discussed in our society is the honesty (or dishonesty) of salespeople. A truly professional salesperson would have great difficulty becoming a con artist or perpetrator of criminal fraud. The professional sales representative knows how important truthfulness is in human relationships. I once was asked to testify as a witness in an antitrust lawsuit. The judge asked the jury members to disregard the fact that I was a salesperson because she didn't want that to influence their verdict. She actually implied that special consideration should be given to a witness if his or her occupation was sales.

This whole issue of truthfulness in sales reminds me of a paradox. There is a hangman who stands on a hill along a road to town. Every person who passes is asked the same question: "Where are you going?" If the passerby answers honestly, he or she is allowed to continue. If he or she tells a lie, he or she will be hanged. There is, however, a reply for which the hangman can neither hang the person nor let the person go. What do you suppose that reply is?

"I have come here so that you may hang me." It is now unfair for the hangman to hang the traveler, for the traveler has told the hangman the truth. Yet, if the hangman lets the traveler go, the traveler's response becomes a *lie*.

Sales professionals sometimes are caught in the middle, trying to balance the interests of their employers and principals with those of their customers and themselves. Sometimes conflicts arise that appear irreconcilable. You receive word that a new model hair dryer is coming out in one month. It is significantly better than the one you are selling now, and it will cost less money. How can you sell the remaining models in stock in good conscience? You could lie and say nothing about the new models to your prospects and customers, or you could explore some other, safer possibilities.

The real sales professionals never trade short-term gains for long-term business relationships. The means to dispose of the old models are numerous. Ask your company to barter the old models for other products that they need. Donate the old models to a worthwhile charity for the tax benefits. Sell the remaining inventory on a clearance basis to a distributor. Sell the remaining models to a beauty school where the new model's features are insignificant. There may be foreign buyers who are interested. Explore your options and turn your sales problems into opportunities. Never, under any circumstances, violate your customer's trust.

THE JAPANESE FORMULA

There is much we can learn from the Japanese, and much they could learn from us. For some Japanese salespersons, the road to success involves a trip to "Hell Camp." In June of 1987, I visited "Hell Camp" in Japan. I purchased the rights to bring this world-famous sales school to the United States. After going through a condensed version of the program, I hired some extraordinary sales trainers to go through the entire thirteen-day sales training program so that they could return to the United States and conduct the training program for salespeople in the United States. The following are excerpts from a report that one instructor filed with me on his return from Japan.

The school is named Kanrisha Yosei Gakko, meaning training school for managers. It enjoys the reputation of being Japan's number-one sales management training school. The school was featured on CBS's "60 Minutes" with Diane Sawyer. The school's first course was introduced in June 1979. This challenging course is called "Hell Camp." To date, more than 80,000 students have graduated from the thirteen-day residential training. Few Westerners have taken the course. Only six Americans have been enrolled in the course, three of whom did not complete it. Only three Americans finished with top honors and went on to earn instructor status.

The course focuses on five main sales areas including problem solving and execution. The market for the school is sales managers. They train seventeen hours a day for thirteen consecutive days or longer. The course is designed to return sales managers to their job sites with a kamikaze-type attitude toward duty, loyalty to company, and devotion to benefiting the group rather than the individual. The course emphasizes humility and attention to details under applied stress. Students are given "ribbons" at the beginning of the course. Some journalists have referred to these ribbons as "ribbons of shame," but actually fourteen ribbons represent tests that must be passed to graduate. The tests include thirteen-mile and twenty-five-mile night hikes in the mountains, memorization and presentation of three long speeches, problem solving of managerial-type problems, physical exercises, and many more. Each time a student passes a test, the corresponding ribbon can be removed. Once the test is passed, any written materials or notes are collected. At any time thereafter, the student can be given a "pop quiz." If the student fails the quiz, he or she regains the ribbon.

The pace of the training is set to stretch every student's abilities to maximum capacity. Official testing begins on the fourth day and covers the information taught and memorized over the first few days. New information is introduced daily, so if a student falls behind in passing the tests, he or she will be juggling more information than the senses can handle at one time. It is not uncommon for a student to be memorizing two speeches and solutions to problems at one time, to keep on top of the training.

There is no time for anything other than study. The day begins at 4:00 A.M. with wake-up/clean-up duties. Formation is at 5:00 A.M. Each day begins with calisthenics and singing exercises. Students are kept occupied with training and testing until 9:30 P.M. Meals average fifteen minutes. The 200-plus students are divided into smaller classes of fifteen. There are two instructors per class.

Everything is done as a group—eating, bathing, studying, memorization, etc. The course demands that each student obey the rules of courtesy. Should one student fail to follow the proper protocol for testing, the entire group is penalized.

At the end of each day, each student writes a report to send to his or her company. The report details how the student will use the day's training when he or she returns to the job. The instructors are in contact with the students' employers on a regular basis to discuss the students' progress. The relationship between the students' companies and the school is very close. Prior to the students' arrival, the school receives employee training profiles from the companies. These profiles give the instructor information that will assist him or her in training the employees.

Having gone through the course myself, the kamikaze attitude is easy to understand. Japanese managers are using the same principles today as those that have been taught throughout Japanese history. They demonstrate an incredible persistence toward *completing* rather than competing. Their sense of competition is built around the benefit to the group versus the individual. Saving face within the group is top priority.

Of the 203 students in the course that my instructor attended, only twenty-one students met the requirements for graduation on the thirteenth day: removal of all the ribbons. Only *eleven* were ready when the ceremony began at 5:00 P.M. Testing continued during the ceremony, so by the end of the formal presentation, more had qualified. This process of testing and graduation continues each day until the sixteenth day. If a student has not passed all the tests by the sixteenth day, he or she is returned to his or her company. Not passing could mean the end to any advancement potential within the company.

Companies send their employees to this school for three main reasons. First, if an employee is moving into a sales management position, the training received at the school will prepare the employee for his or her new role and responsibilities. Second, a company will send a manager who has grown soft in his or her position. For this type of employee, the school offers an opportunity to become remotivated and make a greater contribution to the company. Much of Japanese management philosophy concerns an attitude toward prosperity. A common Japanese fear is that prosperity leads to less productivity, something the Japanese see in American management. Third, a company will send a sales manager who is very close to losing his or her job. If this employee fails the course, he or she will have no future with the company in a sales management position.

To what can I attribute the phenomenal success of Japanese salespersons? Based on my observations while I attended the school, I'd have to say that it's their kamikaze-like attitude toward getting business; their team-effort approach toward serving customers; their loyalty to their companies, their products, and their fellow employees; and a real dedication to completing any task that they are assigned.

THE SECRET REVEALED

It's near the end of the book and I almost forgot to tell you the secret to sales success. Remember the story of the American soldier in Chapter 13, "Can You Make Stone Soup?"

If the hungry soldier had *offered* a way for the villagers to obtain food instead of asking for food when he was knocking on doors, the doors would have been opened wide and he would have been invited in. Once inside, he could have taught the families how to make stone soup. He then would have become a consultative salesperson. The families needed food and he could have shown them how to get it, whereupon they would have networked by inviting friends, family, and neighbors over to contribute to and enjoy the delicious stone soup, which could be prepared in large kettles instead of a small helmet.

The salesperson-soldier could have formed a cooperative food-bank program among the families, and everyone (including himself) would have had food to share throughout the rough times. Nearby towns could have been brought into the program, and a full-fledged barter system could have been implemented. The salesperson-soldier could have analyzed who the Assertive people were and assigned them leadership responsibilities. The Friendly people could have recruited participants, the Analytical types could have kept track of the food contributions, and the Persuasive people could have worked on program development and expansion. The people with Situational personalities could have filled in wherever needed. In short, the entire outcome of the soldier's visit to that little French village would have been dramatically different if he had used the tools described in this book.

After my heart attack, I started a magazine for heart-disease patients. I brought together a printer, artists, editors, writers, sales agents, advertisers, and readers for the common good. I made stone soup.

When I sold windmills, I brought together manufacturing personnel, financial planners, stockbrokers, construction companies, bankers, and investors to make stone soup.

When I sold security-guard services, I brought together security guards, specialized training personnel, and hospital administrators for the common good. Again, I made stone soup.

Whatever you are doing, wherever you are doing it, however you are doing it, you can make stone soup, too. *The ability to create stone soup is the secret to becoming the most successful salesperson in the world.* If you analyze what Lee Iacocca did with Chrysler, what Ted Turner did with CNN, what H. Ross Perot did with EDS, what Conrad Hilton did with the Hilton Hotels, and what thousands of incredibly successful salespeople all over the world have done, you would know that had any of them been that soldier, they would not have been begging—they would have been *selling.*

One of the questions I found myself asking that night in the emergency room on March 3, 1985, was why didn't the soldier sell food instead of beg? Most people would argue that he had nothing to sell, but he did. He had the *knowledge* to create food. That knowledge is more important than the food itself. You can eat a great meal one day and be hungry the next. If you know how to sell, you and those who do business with you always will have a full bowl.

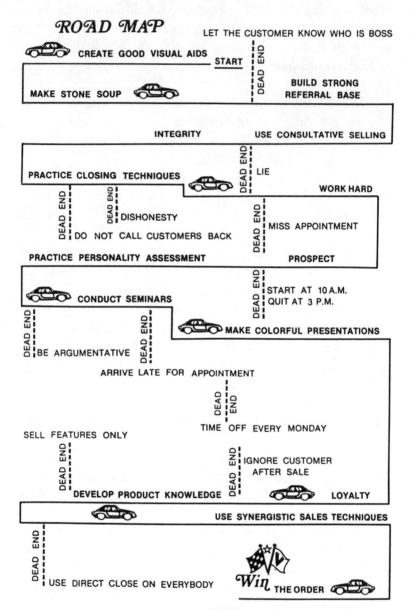

21
A Final Word

This is a big, consuming world we live in, with billions of people consuming millions of products each and every day. You may recall in Chapter 2, "Sales: A Commonsense Career Choice" that I told the story of the two shoe salespeople who went to India. One returned home dejected because he could not find a single customer. The other saw every Indian as a potential customer. The supersalespeople recognize their sales opportunities and use their sales skills to become master sales professionals by selling millions of dollars worth of products and services.

Except for those totalitarian countries in the world where everyone watches the same model of television set and uses the same type of refrigerator, most things are bought and sold in a free market where the basic concept of supply and demand dictates pricing and availability of products and services. Someone is going to earn the commissions, the overrides, the bonuses, the big salaries. If you take your blinders off, set your goals slightly higher than you think are achievable, and employ the techniques revealed in this book, you will succeed and prosper. If you remember that the most important thing in the whole world is to make delicious, hot stone soup, you can become one of the most successful salespeople in the world today.

You can draw a line about thirty-five miles long with an average pencil on a smooth, nonabrasive surface. Although I use my computer for everything else, I write books the old-fashioned way. I have used almost ten pencils while writing this book, so my hand has traveled approximately 350 miles. My mind, on the other hand, has traveled through a lifetime of sales experiences, disappointments, and victories. Danish physicist Niels Bohr reportedly said, "An expert is a man who has made all the mistakes which can be made in a very narrow field." I hope this book will enable you to capitalize on my experiences and re-create the victories without living through the tragedies. Good things come from tragedy, too; I might not have written this book if I hadn't had my heart attack. I hope you have enjoyed reading it as much as I have enjoyed writing it.

As I was writing the conclusion to this book, I received a call from Jeannie Graves whom I mentioned earlier. An English major in college, she started her business out of her home in 1974 with very little working capital. Her great communications skills created a $6-million business with 140 employees and seven sales representatives. In our conversation, Jeannie remarked that a sales call is like a dance. A salesperson takes the lead from the prospect and responds to his or her every move. Let the prospect talk about his or her business, problems, and successes while you take notes. The prospect will be impressed with the fact that you care enough about his or her comments, so be quiet and listen carefully. Be responsive, as a dancer moving with his or her partner. If you really listen, the prospect will tell you what he or she wants. When he or she tells you, close the sale. It's just like dancing, and it's just as much fun.

Jeannie keeps up with industry changes, insists on good customer service, and is principle based. Jeannie asked me to send her a copy of this book, a request that reiterated why she is one of the most successful salespeople in the world: She still has a constant thirst for knowledge despite her great success (not because she requested a copy of my book). The most profound thoughts, the greatest intellectual insights, the most important pieces of information, all are worthless if they are not read, not taught, and not learned.

Opening your eyes to the real sales opportunities is the first and most important step toward becoming a successful salesperson. The second step is to ignore the doomsayers and skeptics who are unable to take their blinders off. Consider what just a few of the naysayers in the past 150 years have said:

1839—Dr. Alfred Velpeau:

"The abolishment of pain in surgery is impossible. It is absurd to go on seeking it today. Knife and pain are two words in surgery that must forever be associated in the consciousness of the patient."

1926—Lee De Forest (inventor of the radio):

"While theoretically and technically television may be feasible, commercially and financially I consider it impossible."

1825—The Quarterly Review
(a prestigious publication):

"What can be more palpably absurd than the prospect held out of locomotives traveling twice as fast as stage coaches?"

1897—Popular Science magazine:

"As a means of rapid transit, flying could not begin to compete with the railroad."

These beliefs were all held by individuals who were greatly respected in their time. Their conclusions were based on limited knowledge and on an inability to take their blinders off and consider the possibilities.

Do you think that you can earn millions of dollars selling? I think you can. Place your trust in yourself and in your abilities. May each and every sales call result in an order. May every order bring prosperity. May prosperity bring you happiness. May happiness bring you peace.

If you want me to review and comment on your work assignments, or if you have any questions, address your correspondence to me at the address that follows. Or write to me and just let me know how you are doing. I would like to add your name to the growing list of multimillionaire sales professionals!

Charles R. Whitlock
2899 Agoura Road, Suite 316
Westlake Village, CA 91361

Appendix A
What Your Travel Agent Won't
Tell You About Business Travel

*"Travel is educational. It teaches you that
enough luggage is too much."*

— Unknown

Many people go into sales because of the travel opportunities, while others go into sales despite the travel required.
This appendix is intended to help make your business
travel as pleasant, comfortable, and inexpensive as possible, whether you have a propensity for traveling or not.

For a short period of time, I sold medical products in
Italy. My employer would provide the airline tickets and a
cash advance. The cash advance equaled $1,000 for each
week of anticipated travel. Usually, my trips would last
for two weeks, so I received a $2,000 cash advance in the
form of traveler's checks.

I've found that whether you earn $50,000 a year or
$100,000, you'll spend that amount to live. Just as every-
one seems to adjust their standards of living to the amount
of their paychecks, I *always* spent my advance, no matter
how long I traveled! If my trip lasted only one week, I still
used up the two-week cash advance.

Salespeople can be pretty strange animals. I do not mean to imply that there was any impropriety, because there was not. It was simply that if I had more money than time, I ate at better restaurants, drank older wines, entertained customers in a more grandiose style, rented more luxurious cars, and bought first-class train seats. If I thought I would be staying a little longer and wanted to stretch my money, I could have stayed a month with only a two-week cash advance.

The company's accountant, on the other hand, would take a $500 cash advance for each week of anticipated travel and *always* return with money that he did not use. He would buy books such as *How to Travel in Europe on $8 a Day* and then actually do what the books suggested!

TO SAVE, PLAN AHEAD

Management-consulting firm Runzheimer International reports that the average out-of-state business trip in 1990 cost $1,023. An American Express Travel Management Services spokesperson estimates that in 1991, air-travel costs will increase as much as 13 percent. Air travel now accounts for as much as 55 percent of all business travel costs. It's projected that by the end of 1991 lodging costs will increase from 4 to 6 percent, car rental cost increases are projected to run 3 to 5 percent, and the cost of meals should increase only 2 percent. Yet, sales and marketing personnel have to be out in the field.

Because of rising costs, Runzheimer reports a decline in the amount of business travel taken over the past few years. Companies have begun to enforce travel policies and seek out cheaper air fares, less expensive lodging, and economy car rentals. Some corporations are enforcing frequent-flier policies that state that all earned mileage reverts back to the corporation. In addition, many companies are negotiating air-fare rates for frequently traveled routes as well as to meetings and conventions. Discretionary travel is being eliminated, and ceilings are being imposed on the amount of reimbursement for meals and lodging.

Whether you are like me or the accountant, you should plan your travel in advance. Not only will you save a great deal of money, but you will find your travel more enjoyable, more productive, and much less hectic.

By planning your business trips well in advance, you will receive the maximum discounts on air travel. At the time of this writing, a commuter flight on a major airline from Los Angeles to San Francisco, round-trip, during the week, without staying over a Saturday night, is about $58 if you book your flight twenty days in advance. If you buy your ticket on the day you intend to travel, that same seat will cost you about $455, almost eight times more money. Although unforeseen events may occur that necessitate last-minute travel, do everything in your power to make such a trip the exception rather than the rule.

Of course, there is a downside to flying inexpensively, and I'm not just talking about the service and quality of meals you receive in coach class versus first class. The inexpensive airline tickets typically are noncancelable, nonrefundable, and nonchangeable. I missed a flight from Chicago to Boston one afternoon, and when I finally made it to the ticket counter to arrange for a later flight, I was informed that I had to throw my tickets in the garbage and buy new ones. It would not have been so bad except that I arrived late at the O'Hare terminal in Chicago because a customer forgot about my appointment and I had to wait an extra hour to see him. The ticket agent at the counter could somehow sense my displeasure at the prospect of buying new tickets. Was it the tired, hangdog expression on my face or the expletive that I muttered under my breath that gave away my bad mood? Whatever it was, this intuitive ticket agent began to explain the "flat-tire" rule to me.

Apparently, most airlines stipulate that if you are holding a nonrefundable, noncancelable, and nonchangeable airline ticket and you have a flat tire while en route to the airport, you may take the next flight out if there is a seat available. Well, suffice it to say that it's not just the Internal Revenue Service (IRS) that can make liars of us all. Besides, the whole concept of nonrefundable this and nonchangeable that can be pretty ridiculous if you ask me.

I did discover one small problem with the flat-tire rule on my way to Los Angeles from Denver one night. I had a couple of glasses of wonderful cabernet sauvignon with an old friend while we sat and talked. I decided to allow the spirits to wear off before driving to the airport. I missed my flight as a result, and shortly after my arrival at the airport, it closed down. The next flight to Los Angeles was at 6:20 the next morning, so I stayed at a nearby hotel.

When I arrived at the airport the next day for the 6:20 A.M. flight, I was told that I had to purchase another ticket because the flat-tire rule is good for only three hours. I could feel my blood pressure start to rise and my face flush. After explaining that I actually had arrived at the airport within the three-hour cutoff only to find that the airport was closed, I begrudgingly bought a new ticket. I guess every loophole has its own loophole.

TRAVEL PRIVILEGES

As a frequent traveler, you can enjoy certain travel privileges by patronizing the same airlines, hotels, and car-rental companies. If you're a very frequent traveler, you may qualify for personalized "power cards." Most airline power cards require a minimum number of miles traveled the previous year, and annual qualifications require continued loyalty and patronage.

Examine the mileage that you earned during the past year and see which airline(s) you used most. Would qualifying for that airline's power card make it easier for you to travel to your destinations of choice? Qualifications and benefits vary by airline but range from bonus mileage, first-class upgrades, and elimination of travel blackouts to automobile rentals, hotel certificates, and priority wait-listing.

Also available are hotel power cards from many major chains that offer the opportunity to earn bonus points and receive room-upgrade certificates and upgrades on arrival. Marriott, Hilton, Hyatt, Sheraton, Ramada, Westin, and Holiday Inn are some of the hotel chains that offer membership cards.

Avis, National, and Hertz are among the best-known car-rental companies offering the benefits of membership. Probably the greatest benefit is your ability to go directly to your rental car without having to check in at the counter. Membership requirements vary from a straight annual fee to a minimum rental frequency. Find out which company gives you the best corporate rate and if any have arrangements with the airlines you use frequently to contribute frequent-flier points.

If you fly a great deal, you may be interested in joining the American European Travel Marketing Group (AETMG) as an independent travel agent. AETMG will give you or your company a rebate of 20 percent of the commissions it earns on the travel you book with AETMG through its 800 toll-free number. Because the travel agency normally receives a 10 percent commission from the airlines, if you travel a lot, your quarterly rebate could be a nice bonus. AETMG has offices all over the world. Write to me at 2899 Agoura Road, Suite 316, Westlake Village, CA 91361, and I will forward your request to the AETMG office nearest to you.

PLAN YOUR APPOINTMENTS WELL

When traveling by air, always allow plenty of time to adjust to the time difference when you reach your destination. Flying west to east can be particularly difficult. I can leave Los Angeles at noon and arrive in New York at 9:30 P.M. An hour later (7:30 P.M. Los Angeles time), I am in my hotel room struggling to go to sleep because I know that I've got a breakfast meeting with a very important prospective customer. I never go to bed before 11:00 P.M. in Los Angeles, so I end up reading a book until 2:00 A.M. My wake-up call comes at 6:30 A.M. and I am totally exhausted the rest of the day.

If at all possible, arrange your first appointment the day after your arrival to allow for the possibility of experiencing jet lag. Your mind and body will appreciate the good night's sleep and you'll be much more effective.

Flying east to west is not nearly so bad a strain on my system. By leaving New York at noon, you can arrive in Los Angeles by about 3:00 P.M. on a nonstop flight. You can enjoy a great dinner in the early evening and still get a good night's sleep. Flying east to west across the country just seems a lot more civilized.

What if you are forced to take the red-eye flight because of an emergency or a last-minute trip? Late-night travel offers a few advantages. Usually, the airlines will give you a little better rate. If you travel on the red-eye specials, you will have more time to make sales calls during normal business hours. The lack of sleep, problems finding a taxi at three in the morning, and having to find another hotel at four in the morning because your confirmed reservation was lost, however, far outweigh the advantages, in my opinion. Work from 9:00 A.M. to 5:00 P.M. and travel from 6:00 P.M. to 10:00 P.M., if at all possible. Unless it is an absolute necessity, do not travel from 10:00 P.M. to 6:00 A.M. Whatever savings you may get on your airline tickets you may relinquish in medical bills.

If you're making calls in an unfamiliar city, pick up a map in advance of your arrival and locate your prospects' addresses on the map. Your challenge will be to arrange your schedule so that you drive the least possible distance. Make your first sales call at the location that is farthest from your hotel (unless a dinner appointment makes this plan inadvisable). Use noncustomer time when possible (before 9:00 A.M. and after 5:00 P.M.) to travel. Methodically make your return to your hotel without going back and forth across town. Allow a little extra time between appointments for the *remote* possibility of getting lost or turned around in the city.

PACKING

If you carry samples or literature, or have a tangible product to demonstrate, you may want to have these materials carefully boxed and shipped to your hotel in advance of your arrival so that you won't have to carry them on the plane. If you rent a car once you land, the boxes could come in handy as file organizers in the trunk of your car.

Purchase a good carry-on bag and avoid checking your baggage with the airlines at all costs. Every well-traveled businessperson has experienced the personal hell of arriving in a city for an important engagement with no clothes to wear because his or her baggage took a detour through the "Twilight Zone." Somewhere floating around Vancouver, British Columbia, there still is a piece of luggage containing four days' worth of my clothes. And all my audiovisual aids disappeared in Cleveland one disastrous trip, never to be seen again. I've lost luggage all over the world, so I've learned never to check baggage unless I have to.

If you are going on an extended sales trip, take some time to really plan your wardrobe. Take a minimum of clothing but make sure it is all well coordinated. If I wear a gray suit and pack a black suit and four shirts, I have four possible combinations (each of the suits, the black trousers with the gray jacket, the gray trousers with the black jacket). Plus, I need only one pair of black shoes. Men still have an unfair advantage over women in this arena, because it's acceptable for men to wear the same suit more than once on a business trip, but many women still feel uncomfortable "repeating" an outfit. Whether you're male or female, if you have a problem coordinating clothing or can't resist the urge to pack virtually every stitch of clothing you own, ask a good friend or wardrobe consultant to assist you in your planning.

If you have scheduled a business trip lasting more than one week, just pack one week's worth of clothing. Periodically, take your dirty clothing to a local laundry. Even with one-day service, it shouldn't cost you an arm and a leg. Speaking of money, don't use the hotel laundry service unless money is not important to you or your company. On one trip to New York, the hotel where I was staying wanted $3 a pair to wash my socks! Luckily, dress socks were on sale at a nearby department store for three pairs for $10. I bought a lot of socks that trip. If my books stop selling, I think I've found a way to make a lot of money: open a sock-washing business for hotels.

ONCE YOU GET THERE

When you arrive at your hotel, hang your clothes up as soon as possible. If your shirts or blouses are wrinkled, ask room service to bring you an iron and ironing board. Most of the better hotels will provide irons, ironing boards, hair dryers, and toiletry kits if you've forgotten your toothbrush or razor blades.

The first night on my arrival in a hotel I usually run the bathwater at its hottest setting after taking a shower. Then I close the door and spend ten to fifteen minutes breathing the hot steam. The hot steam helps soothe your vocal cords and relieve your travel tensions (and it can help take the wrinkles out of your clothes). Always pack cough drops, drink plenty of water, and take care of your vocal cords because you'll probably be using them a great deal during your trip. Remember that it would be pretty hard to sell without your voice. Rest your voice in the evening as much as possible. If you are going to make frequent presentations, drink plenty of water throughout each presentation. Sometimes when in a foreign environment, people forget to do the things that they naturally would do at home, like taking good care of themselves. Stay at a hotel with a physical fitness room so you can work off any extra calories that you may consume on business trips.

AETMG can arrange for hotel discounts, or you can ask your company to contact the major chains to negotiate national discounts, if it hasn't already arranged for corporate rates. Usually, hotels charge a higher rate for those who travel Monday through Friday, so if you have to stay over a weekend, ask for the lower weekend rate. Do not assume that the hotel automatically will give you the lower rate. Frequently, hotels offer their weekend guests discount-coupon packages that often include drinks and meals in the hotel.

Often, the closer a hotel is to an airport or the downtown area, the higher its rate. If you are going to rent a car, you might want to consider finding a hotel close to the locations of your next day's sales calls. If you are not going to rent a car, a $10 taxi ride can be easily justified when you save $50 to $80 a night on your hotel bill by staying in less-expensive areas.

If you must rent a car, there are a few things you should consider. Comparison shop because there are differences between the auto-rental companies. If you plan on driving a lot in a short period of time, you may be better off with an unlimited mileage/high daily rate rental program. If your sales calls will be primarily in the city and you do not plan on driving a lot, you may want to go with the low daily rate and pay a mileage fee. Discounts are available from many sources. Your company may have negotiated a corporate discount for its employees. If you belong to an auto club, a civic or fraternal organization, a discount buyers' group, the National Association of the Self-Employed, or another professional organization, inquire about any auto-rental discounts that they may have arranged for their members. If you become an independent agent with AETMG, you will be entitled to 10 to 30 percent auto-rental discounts at some agencies.

Check with your employer and your insurance agent to see if you need to purchase the additional insurance offered by the car-rental agency. I normally don't take the additional insurance coverage because my own automobile insurance covers me while I am driving a rental car. Don't waste your money buying something that you do not need. Although most policies have exclusions and limits on certain property, your home-owner's insurance probably protects you against theft of any personal property stolen from your rental car. When someone broke into a car I was renting and stole six one-ounce gold bars, my insurance company reimbursed me for only two of them. My employer's insurance covered the remaining four bars. Ask your employer and your personal insurance agent about the coverage you have. If you feel you need more, perhaps you can purchase it and pass the cost along to your employer. A word to the wise: Always lock your samples and materials in the trunk. An attaché case on the backseat is an open invitation to a thief.

Whenever you rent a car, check the miles on the odometer against the miles indicated on your paperwork. It took me twenty minutes in Washington, D.C., to convince the woman at the car-rental counter that I could not possibly have driven 840 miles in the four hours that I was in possession of the car. We mutually agreed on 140 miles. If I had only checked the odometer when I rented the car, I would have noticed the 700-mile discrepancy. Also check for dents, scratches, or broken windows. If you find any, have an employee acknowledge the defect on the rental agreement before you leave. Such an annoyance always seems to cost a few dollars *less* than the deductible amount on your insurance policy, so you end up paying for it. Finally, make sure there is a spare tire and a jack in the trunk and that everything works, including the lights, air conditioner, and heater.

One final word on auto rentals: Try not to rent a car in one city and return it in another city because dropoff fees can be more than the price of an airplane ticket. If you must pick up a car in one city and drop it off in another, comparison shop the major auto-rental companies for the best bargains. I've found, for example, that if you rent a car from a company-owned outlet in Salt Lake City, Utah, and return the car to a company-owned outlet in Portland, Oregon, the cost is approximately $250. If you rent the same car from an authorized franchise dealer and return it to another franchise dealership or a company-owned outlet, the cost jumps to $670. It pays to do some investigating.

STAY IN TOUCH WITH YOUR OFFICE

Keep on top of your work at home while you're on the road. In this terrific age of communication, there's no reason to be in the dark about what's going on in your office while you're away. Take advantage of overnight mail, facsimile machines, electronic mail, and voice-mail systems. If these services are unavailable where you are, have your mail and messages delivered to you at your hotel on a regular basis (such as every other day). If you are working on the West Coast, wake up a little early and make your calls to the East Coast. If you are working on the East Coast, you can return your telephone messages at the end of your workday.

In the evenings, go through your mail and write your responsive correspondence. When you return to your office, you won't have two weeks of work waiting for you. More important, you won't have missed any sales opportunities. Imagine this: It's your first day back in the office. As you're sifting through the volumes of unopened mail, you find an urgent fax from a customer you've been pursuing for six months. He asks you for a quotation within five business days: his supplier's manufacturing plant burned to the ground and left him high and dry. If you are nonresponsive, he will be forced to buy from abroad. The order was virtually dropped in your lap, but you blew it.

A FEW TIPS

These days the IRS requires receipts for everything. Use charge cards wherever and whenever possible. Your monthly statements will serve as proof of payments. I have had hotels bill me twice for the same stay, so get your receipts and hang on to them! If you haven't marked the names of your clients on the charge receipts, write the names beside the item on the bill once you receive it. Get receipts for everything. If you are self-employed, the IRS will want to see them if you are ever audited. If you work for someone else and turn in travel and entertainment reports, your employer will retain your receipts in case it is audited. If you use your own car to conduct business, write down the starting and ending odometer readings each day. These records, coupled with your gas receipts, should provide you with all the record keeping you will need to take your auto-expense deductions. Check with your company's accounting department, tax department, or your CPA for specific details and recommendations about record keeping and tax deductions.

The more planning you do, the more fun and productive your traveling will be. Take advantage of your travels and visit tourist attractions while there. Most cities have a great deal to see and enjoy. Whether it's museums, zoos, wild-animal parks, nighttime entertainment, historic architecture and monuments, or wining and dining at a special restaurant, soak up the local color. Experience the beauty of each city you visit and enjoy its people. I owe a lifetime of fabulous travel experiences to my sales career, and I wouldn't change any of it for the world.

Appendix B
What Sales and Marketing Software Are the Professionals Using?

"The computer is a great invention. There are as many mistakes as ever, but now they're nobody's fault."

—Unknown

There are more than 600 sales software programs available to help you manage your sales and marketing information better. If you can reduce the amount of time you spend handling administrative duties, you can devote more time to your prospects and customers.

SELECTING A SOFTWARE PACKAGE

When selecting a sales-and-marketing software package, you should consider the software's purpose, the ability to customize the software, its upgradability, its cost, and the reputation of its manufacturer.

If you are calling on fifty hospitals in downtown New York and selling only one product, your software needs probably will be minimal. If, on the other hand, you work for a distributor and sell 2,000 products to 4,000 retail stores in a three-state territory, you will need a more-sophisticated software package. If you are a sales manager and are responsible for forty sales representatives in nine states and you cover a handful of house accounts, you will require yet another software package.

Functionality is the key to buying a sales-and-marketing software program. Identify what your needs are first. Do you need a way to track leads? What about call reporting? Perhaps you need access to maintenance and service reports. What problems are you having now that a software program could help you resolve? What would make your life easier and your commissions increase? Carefully consider your needs, the needs of management, and the needs of your customers before you purchase.

You'll probably want a software program that will enable you to keep complete account-record files with names, addresses, dates of sales calls, cross-references to correspondence files, action dates with red-flag reminders, territory management, sales forecasting, note history, and word processing. If price is not a major factor, you may want to consider a software package that interacts with a relational database for greater flexibility. This distributed system usually is compatible with many hardware systems and information can be transferred easily between the field sales offices and the home office or between field sales offices.

When selecting a sales software package, one consideration is whether or not you can adapt the software to your personal needs and routines. Also consider the upgradability because you'll want to add new technology to your existing package at some time. It's important, too, that modular packages are compatible with your other software.

Make sure that you understand the true cost of the program. Does the price include the necessary training and support you'll need? Are upgrades included? In general, the more you want, the more you will have to pay. It's up to you to determine and then buy only what you need.

One of the great benefits of many of these software products is that they come in modular form so that you can buy the modules as you need them. One such sales software program is the TeleSell Sales Information System manufactured by TeLeVell Sales Solutions (1629 S. Main St., Milpitas, CA 95035, [408] 956-0511, fax [408] 956-0202).

TeleSell's system has six basic modules. The Salesperson's module is menu driven and easy to use. This module will allow you to retrieve information on your customers' buying patterns, decision makers, and noteworthy comments from prior sales calls. It also has an on-line tickler file that will remind you to make your next call or to submit a new quotation as the contract year is almost over. It features to-do lists and will qualify leads based on your qualification criteria. Use it to generate instant letters from boilerplate paragraphs; simply select an appropriate opening paragraph, content paragraphs, and closing paragraph. Type in your prospect's or customer's name and address, and your follow-up visit letter, quotation, or general correspondence requirements are set.

The Salesperson module has custom fields, on-line product and competition information, itinerary planning and scheduling, and a security password feature. In short, it has basically everything you need to manage a sales territory effectively.

You can add the Forecasting module that will enable you to forecast sales by product, representative, territory, or division. You can develop dynamic strategies, identify trends, predict sales cycles, and edit your forecasts to compensate for market trends.

TeleSell has an Advertising Manager module for tracking promotion effectiveness and the true value of advertisements that is excellent for determining referral effectiveness. Its Reseller Manager module will enable you to distribute leads to dealers, distributors, or other representatives; it also performs other major functions that will help you manage a dealer sales organization.

The Product Manager module will maintain files on customer interest by product and will enable you to enter your product specifications and even your competitors' specifications and sales information for on-line access. The Remote Update module allows a sales department to distribute data nationwide. This module will send each department only the specified data required for its specific needs.

Sales-cycle modules are available to manage mailing lists, bulk mail, advertising, inquiry handling, telemarketing, sales-call management, dealer management, order entry, and customer service. One concept I particularly like is that with the TeleSell package you can use many of the popular word-processing software packages. The Reporting modules with report writing, forecasting, sales management, and mapmaker capability add a comprehensive sales-management capability. The Communications modules include call routing, fax interface, remote update, and sales E-mail (sending messages via computer) capability for managing your sales office. With Accounting Interface, you can flag accounts receivable, commission payments, and accounts payable, if applicable.

Each of the TeleSell modules are priced at approximately $495 for a single user. Companies can buy the modules for approximately $2,000 with a four-person user base. Each additional person added to the system will cost about $200.

At the end of this appendix, I have listed several reputable software manufacturers whose sales and marketing software is competitively priced. Discuss your software needs with the Management Information System (MIS) department in your company, and ask associates and other sales professionals for their recommendations. Call or write each company and ask for a videotape, literature, and the names of any customers in your area whom you can call for information about how the products work for them.

Take the time to shop around. The software manufacturer you select should be knowledgeable about sales and marketing functions as well as computer software. The manufacturer should provide appropriate training and customer support. Make sure that the software addresses the need for market analysis and customer data in addition to providing administrative tools. It should meet the needs not only of sales and marketing staff members, but also of top management, sales and marketing management, and customers.

PERSONAL COMPUTER PRIMER

Salespeople have discovered that the computer is as crucial to their success as the telephone, calculator, copier, fax machine, or file cabinet. The computer can perform all of these functions and more, and a personal computer (PC) is ideal for managing a sales territory.

The PC used to be a luxury; today, it is a necessity. Your quotations (and other sales documents) may be transmitted by computer. You can talk to your home office by computer with the use of a modem. With a word-processing program and a printer, you can easily generate all of your own correspondence.

For many of you, the computer still may be a mystery. A computer is nothing more than an information processor. You can store, retrieve, delete, chart, compare, analyze, project, and communicate with a computer, frequently performing these feats at lightning speed. Think of computer hardware (processor) as an engine. The processor has a microchip that is the brain of the computer. It contains memory and controls the information flow within the computer. It processes information as *bits*, which come in as electrical impulses and leave as reports, letters, or whatever form you want. Processors generally come in eight-, sixteen-, or thirty-two-*bit* sizes, which you can equate to horsepower. The larger the bit size, the faster the computer. A computer's processing also is affected by its internal clock. A four-megahertz clock is faster than a two-megahertz clock, for example.

The computer's memory determines the size of the jobs it can do. Computer memories are expressed in *byte* (not *bit*) sizes. A *byte* is eight *bits*, the minimum amount of information a computer needs to form a letter or a number. Desktop computer memories used for business purposes range from 640,000 *bytes*—640K for short—up to 16 million *bytes*, or sixteen *megabytes* (MB). The average-size memory you will require for management of a sales territory is one to two *megabytes*.

Visit local, reputable computer stores that carry IBM, Toshiba, Macintosh, NEC, Compaq, and other national brands of PCs. There is a wealth of IBM-compatible equipment available, and you should consider the option of putting together your own system. Many retail stores carry several product lines that will give you the ability to do some serious comparison shopping.

Once you have selected a PC, you will need to evaluate peripheral equipment, which includes keyboards, input devices such as the mouse, monitors, printers, and modems. You can spend as much money on the peripherals as you can spend on the PC itself, so evaluate your need for these devices carefully. Color monitors and color printers are available that can make a sales presentation spectacular. Many popular consumer periodicals annually rate the latest PC equipment, so check your library for more specific information about selection.

If you select the right PC or laptop computer (portable computer), you can conduct your sales business more efficiently, more effectively, and more innovatively. As you work for efficiency and effectiveness, you'll find you've liberated the most precious resource of all in the world of sales: time. The additional time to prospect more intensively, time to make more presentations, and time to manage your territory probably will give you a payback on your hardware and software in no time at all. You (your company or your boss) can justify buying your system by simply looking at the features and corresponding benefits of a PC and the proper sales and marketing software.

Feature	Benefit
To increase sales	
Automatically update sales analysis	React to sales trends
Automatic back-order handling	Reduce lost sales
To increase profits	
Input invoicing information with profit data	Focus on profitable customers and items
On-line credit checking	Reduce bad debt
Daily sales recap	Reduce pricing errors and concessions
Invoices on demand	Reduce the billing-cycle time and get paid faster
Automatic editing and corrections	Reduce errors
Automatic order writing and billing	Reduce clerical costs
Automatic updating of accounts receivable	Quicker billing cycle

If you calculate the increased sales benefits and the increased profit benefits, the decision of whether or not to buy a PC should be an easy one. When you shop for your PC, tell the sales representative your needs and what you want a PC to do. He or she then can demonstrate hardware systems that will meet your specific needs. Many of the computer stores offer training programs. If they do not, they probably can refer you to a school in the area that does. If not, contact the manufacturer for a list of authorized training schools in your area.

WHAT ABOUT A LAPTOP COMPUTER?

Many of today's portable computers have become as sophisticated as full-sized PCs. Whether for use in the office or out in the field, laptops are great. Models run anywhere from small computers like the Tandy 102 with only 32K of memory that's perfect for correspondence and notes to the 16-pound Macintosh portable that will run for ten hours on a single battery charge. Other popular models include the Compaq Lte, the NEC UltraLite, and the Toshiba T1000SE. It's wise to shop around for the best price, and always check out the sales!

A laptop model that is clearly one of the hardware systems of choice for the traveling sales professional is the AST Premium Exec 386SX/20 Notebook Computer. This is a 6½-pound notebook computer that fits in a standard briefcase with room left over for your paperwork. It measures 11.4" × 9" × 2.25" and comes with a tilt stand for a comfortable typing position. It has 40 MB of fast access hard drive, is battery- or line cord-driven, has loads of built-in interfaces, and optional modems are available. You can attach a printer like the Canon BJ-10e Bubble Jet printer and print letterheads, envelopes, and general correspondence virtually anywhere. The printer may be battery-operated and has an optional automatic paper feeder.

You can even buy a fax module and fax directly from your computer/printer.

RESOURCES: SALES AND MARKETING
SOFTWARE COMPANIES

Abend Associates
265 Winn Street
Burlington, MA 01803
(617) 273-5383
Software: Callback sales software

Contact Software International
1625 West Crosby Road, #132
Carrollton, TX 75006
(214) 418-1866
Software: Act! sales software

Creagh Computers
674 Via de La Valle, Suite 204
Solana Beach, CA 92075
(619) 792-1367
Software: BizBase sales software

Eighty/20 Software
P.O. Box 682
Hutchinson, MN 55350
(612) 587-8020
Software: EXPEED sales software

Emis Software
901 NE Loop 410, Suite 526
San Antonio, TX 78209
(512) 822-8499
Software: EMIS sales software

Informatic Group
100 Shield Street
West Hartford, CT 06110
(203) 953-4040
Software: ACT III sales software

TeLeVell Sales Solutions
1629 S. Main St.
Milpitas, CA 95035
(408) 956-0511
Software: TeleSell Sales Solutions

Multiuser Software Programs

Brock Control Systems
2859 Paces Ferry Road, Suite 1000
Atlanta, GA 30339
(404) 431-1200
Software: Brock Activity Manager with 3-user minimum

Coffman Systems
13140 Midway Place
Cerritos, CA 90701
(213) 926-6653
Software: EDGE sales software with 8-user minimum

Intelligent Technology Group
115 Evergreen Heights Drive
Pittsburgh, PA 15229
(412) 931-7600
Software: Intellidesk sales software

Software companies frequently change their software packages, so request information on the latest software version and current prices before ordering.

Resources

ASSOCIATIONS

Advertising and Marketing International Network
(AMIN)
7155 Old Katy Rd.
Bellaire, TX 77401
(713) 666-1765

Founded: 1932. Members: 31. Cooperative nationwide network of noncompeting independent advertising agencies organized to provide facilities and branch office services for affiliated agencies.

American Management Association (AMA)
135 W. 50th St.
New York, NY 10020
(212) 586-8100

Founded: 1923. Members: 75,000. Membership includes managers in industry, commerce, and government; charitable and noncommercial organizations; university teachers of management; and administrators.

American Marketing Association (AMA)
250 S. Wacker Dr., Ste. 200
Chicago, IL 60606
(312) 648-0536

Founded: 1915. Members: 53,000. Professional society of marketing and marketing research executives, sales and promotion managers, advertising specialists, teachers, and others interested in marketing.

American Telemarketing Association (ATA)
5000 Van Nuys Blvd., #400
Sherman Oaks, CA 91403
(818) 995-0905

Founded: 1983. Members: 840. Businesses involved in telephone marketing sales, including suppliers, distributors, users, and hardware and software manufacturers; educators; and telemarketing businesses. Seeks to provide for the specific needs of the total telephone marketing community.

Association for Convention Operations Management (ACOM)
1819 Peachtree St. NE, Ste. 560
Atlanta, GA 30309
(404) 351-3220

ACOM's 500-plus membership includes convention service directors, managers, and coordinators with convention facilities, bureaus, and hotel corporations. Aim: to increase the effectiveness, productivity, and quality of meetings.

Association of Incentive Marketing (AIM)
1600 Route 22, Ste. 300
Union, NJ 07083
(908) 687-3090

Offers basic and advanced seminars for professionals within the industry.

Association of Retail Marketing Services (ARMS)
3 Caro Court
Red Bank, NJ 07701
(908) 842-5070

Focuses on incentive promotion at the retail level, offers legal and legislative services to the industry, conducts research programs, and compiles statistics.

Convention Liaison Council (CLC)
1575 Eye St. NW, Ste. 1200
Washington, DC 20005
(202) 626-2764 or 626-2789

Comprises 22 organizations involved with the convention, meeting, trade show, travel, and tourism industries.

Council of Sales Promotion Agencies (CSPA)
750 Summer St.
Stamford, CT 06901
(203) 325-3911

Founded: 1969. Members: 70. Agencies with a primary interest in sales promotion. Seeks to increase management understanding of sales promotion as a special component of the total marketing management and corporate communication function.

Direct Marketing Association (DMA)
11 W. 42nd St.
New York, NY 10036-8096
(212) 768-7277

Founded: 1917. Members: 6,800. Manufacturers, wholesalers, public utilities, retailers, mail-order firms, publishers, schools, clubs, insurance companies, financial organizations, business equipment manufacturers, paper and envelope manufacturers, list brokers, compilers, managers, owners, computer service bureaus, advertising agencies, lettershops, research organizations, printers, lithographers, creators, and producers of direct mail and direct response advertising. Studies consumer and business attitudes toward direct mail and related direct marketing statistics.

Direct Marketing Insurance Council (DMIC)
c/o Direct Marketing Association
11 W. 42nd St.
New York, NY 10036-8096
(212) 768-7277

Members: 175. Direct response divisions of insurance companies, service companies that work with direct response divisions.

Direct Selling Association (DSA)
1776 K St., NW, Ste. 600
Washington, DC 20006
(202) 293-5760

Founded: 1910. Members: 200. Manufacturers and distributors selling consumer products door-to-door and through home party plans.

Direct Selling Education Foundations (DSEF)
1776 K St., NW, Ste. 600
Washington, DC 20006
(202) 293-5760

Founded: 1973. Nonmembership. Purpose is to serve the public interest in the marketplace. Advocates marketplace ethics, consumer knowledge, and consumer satisfaction.

Exposition Service Contractors Association (ESCA)
Union Station, Ste. 210
400 S. Houston St.
Dallas, TX 75202
(214) 742-9217

Composed of companies that provide materials and/or
services for trade shows and business meetings, such as
booth construction, installation and dismantling, and
audiovisual equipment.

Financial Marketing Association (FMA)
P.O. Box 14167
Madison, WI 53714
(608) 271-2664

Founded: 1983. Members: 710. A division of the Credit
Union Executives Society. Marketing professionals, consultants, credit unions or leagues, and financial institutions
working to promote the interests of financial marketing.

Health Industry Representatives Association (HIRA)
5818 Reeds Dr.
Shawnee Mission, KS 66202
(913) 262-4513

Founded: 1978. Members: 200. Manufacturers' representatives who operate independent marketing firms under contract to manufacturers of noncompeting lines and manufacturers within the health-care industry who market
through independent marketing firms.

Incentive Federation Inc.
P.O. Box 774
Madison Square Station

New York, NY 10159
(no phone)

Acts as the governmental relations arm of promotional marketing professionals.

Incentive Manufacturers Representatives Association (IMRA)
1555 Naperville/Wheaton Rd., Ste. 103B
Naperville, IL 60563
(708) 369-3466

Organized in 1963 to promote the highest professional standards of incentive representation through the education and interaction of its representative and manufacturer members.

International Association of Conference Centers (IACC)
900 S. Highway Dr.
Fenton, MO 63026
(314) 349-5576

Seeks to provide its executive, resort, corporate, college/university, and nonresidential conference and meeting centers with a single industrywide voice.

International Association of Convention & Visitor Bureaus (IACVB)
P.O. Box 758
Champaign, IL 61824
(217) 359-8881

More than 380 member bureaus in 25 countries. Serves as a clearinghouse for meetings information from all of its member cities.

Marketing Communications Executives International
(MCEI)
4901 Woodall St.
Dallas, TX 75247
(214) 631-1150

Founded: 1954. Members: 500. Executives engaged in the
supervision, planning, execution, or direction of marketing
communications; and educators teaching marketing communications.

Marketing Research Association (MRA)
111 E. Wacker Dr., Ste. 600
Chicago, IL 60601
(312) 644-6610

Founded: 1954. Members: 3,000. Companies and individuals involved in any area of marketing research, such as
data collection, research, or as an end user.

Meeting Planners International (MPI)
Infomart Building
1950 Stemmons Freeway
Dallas, TX 75207
(214) 746-5236

Professionals who plan and manage meetings, conferences,
and trade shows, as well as those who provide goods and
services to the meetings industry.

Multi-Level Marketing International Association
(MLMIA)
119 Stanford
Irvine, CA 92715
(714) 854-5488

Founded: 1985. Companies, support groups, and distributors. Seeks to strengthen and improve the multilevel marketing industry in the United States and abroad.

National Account Marketing Association (NAMA)
310 Madison Ave., Ste. 724
New York, NY 10017
(212) 983-5140

Founded: 1964. Members: 325. Corporation sales or marketing executives concerned with national account sales.

National Association of Business and Industrial Saleswomen (NABIS)
90 Corona, Ste. 1407
Denver, CO 80218
(303) 777-7257

Founded: 1980. Women who sell business and industrial
products or services. Facilitates the exchange of ideas and
experiences in an effort to further professional and personal development for women in a male-dominated field.

National Association of Market Developers (NAMD)
1422 W. Peachtree NW, Ste. 300
Atlanta, GA 30309
(404) 892-0244

Founded: 1953. Members: 700. Professionals engaged in
marketing, sales, sales promotion, advertising, or public
relations who are concerned with the delivery of goods and
services to the minority consumer market.

National Association for Professional Saleswomen (NAPS)
P.O. Box 2606
Novato, CA 94948
(415) 898-2606

Founded: 1980. Members: 5,000. Women actively involved or interested in professional sales and marketing careers. Conducts seminars, surveys, and research projects.

National Network of Women in Sales (NNWS)
701 E. Ogden, Ste. 113
Naperville, IL 60563
(800) 321-6697

Founded: 1981. Members: 750. Women who are in sales or a related career or are seeking to enter the field. Furthers the careers of professional saleswomen by providing support and sharing expertise and experience.

National Sales and Marketing Council
c/o National Association of Home Builders of the United States (NAHB)
15th and M Sts., NW
Washington, DC 20005
(202) 822-0200

Members of the NAHB include single- and multifamily home builders, commercial builders, and others associated with the building industry. NAHB maintains the National Sales and Marketing Council.

National Society of Sales Training Executives (NSSTE)
203 E. Third St., Ste. 201
Sanford, FL 32771
(407) 322-3364

Founded: 1940. Members: 145. Corporate directors and managers of sales and marketing training and human resources development.

Private Label Manufacturers Association (PLMA)
369 Lexington Ave.
New York, NY 10017
(212) 972-3131

Founded: 1979. Members: 900. Manufacturers, brokers, wholesalers, retailers, and consultants. Educates consumers on the quality and value of private label or store-brand products.

Promotion Marketing Association of America (PMAA)
322 Eighth Ave., Ste. 1201
New York, NY 10001
(212) 206-1100

Founded: 1911. Members: 500. Promotion service companies, sales incentive organizations, and companies using promotion programs. Associate members are manufacturers of premium merchandise, consultants, and advertising agencies.

Sales and Marketing Executives International (SMEI)
Statler Office Tower #458
Cleveland, OH 44115
(216) 771-6650

Founded: 1935. Members: 10,000. Executives concerned with sales and marketing management, research, training, and other managerial aspects of distribution. Members control activities of 3 million salespersons.

Society for Marketing Professional Services (SMPS)
99 Canal Center Plaza, Ste. 320
Alexandria, VA 22314
(703) 549-6117

Founded: 1973. Members: 3,500. Employees of architectural, engineering, planning, interior design, landscape architectural, and construction management firms who are responsible for the new business development of their companies.

Women in Advertising and Marketing (WAM)
4200 Wisconsin Ave., NW, Ste. 106-238
Washington, DC 20016
(301) 369-7400

Founded: 1980. Members: 225. Professional women in advertising and marketing. Serves as a network to keep members abreast of developments in advertising and marketing.

Women's Direct Response Group—New York Chapter
(WDRG)
224 Seventh St.
Garden City, NY 11530
(212) 744-3506

Founded: 1970. Members: 600. Direct marketing professionals. Seeks to advance the interests and influence of women in the direct response industry.

Women in Sales Association (WIS)
Eight Madison Ave.
P.O. Box M
Valhalla, NY 10595
(914) 946-3802

Founded: 1979. Members: 1,000. Professional saleswomen
and students aspiring to careers in sales. Promotes professional development of women in sales.

World Federation of Direct Selling Associations (WFDSA)
1776 K St., NW, Ste. 600
Washington, DC 20006
(202) 293-5760

Members: 29. International trade associations. Seeks to
facilitate information sharing among members, especially
regarding developments in specific markets.

SOURCES OF TRADE SHOW INFORMATION

Trade Show Bureau
1660 Lincoln St., Ste. 2050
Denver, CO 80264
(303) 860-7626

Acts as resource center. Will help with research and information about trade shows. Produces numerous publications.

Trade Show & Exhibits Schedule
Bill Communications, Inc.
633 Third Ave.
New York, NY 10017

World Meetings, United States and Canada
Macmillan Publishing Co.
866 Third Ave.
New York, NY 10022

MARKETING EDUCATION ORGANIZATIONS

Academy of Marketing Science (AMS)
School of Business Administration
P.O. Box 248012
University of Miami
Coral Gables, FL 33124
(305) 284-6673

Founded: 1971. Members: 1,000. Marketing academicians and practitioners and individuals interested in fostering education in marketing science. Purpose is to promote the advancement of knowledge and the furthering of professional standards in the field of marketing.

Direct Marketing Educational Foundation (DMEF)
11 W. 42nd St.
New York, NY 10017
(212) 768-7277

Founded: 1965. Members: 400. Individuals, firms, and organizations interested in furthering college-level education in direct marketing. Functions as the collegiate arm of the direct marketing profession.

International Marketing Institute (IMI)
314 Hammond St.
Boston College
Chestnut Hill, MA 02167
(617) 552-8690

Founded: 1960. Alumni: 44,400. Marketing executives. Objective is to promote professionalized marketing management skills through six-week summer marketing management program designed to improve the skills of professionals in the field.

Marketing Education Association (MEA)
1375 King Ave., Ste. 1A
Columbus, OH 43212
(800) 448-0398

Founded: 1982. Members: 2,000. Teachers, teacher coordinators, local and state supervisors, teacher educators, researchers, and curriculum specialists. Purposes are to encourage research and to provide leadership for the growth and improvement of teacher education in marketing education at all levels.

Marketing Science Institute (MSI)
1000 Massachusetts Ave.
Cambridge, MA 02138
(617) 491-2060

Founded: 1961. Members: 43. Nonprofit marketing research center. Seeks to improve marketing practice and education by developing theories and techniques that can be applied to understanding and solving current marketing problems.

Marketing and Training Institute (MTI)
888 16th St., NW, 2nd Fl.
Washington, DC 20006
(202) 296-4250

Service organization jointly owned and operated by the Milk Industry Foundation and the International Ice Cream Association. Conducts sales training, management, merchandising, and marketing classes for member firms.

RESEARCH SOURCES

3M Meeting Management Institute
3M Center, A-145-5N-01
Austin, TX 78769-2963
(512) 984-1800

Clearinghouse for information on meetings. Funds meetings research.

University of North Carolina at Chapel Hill
Center for International Marketing
School of Business
Carroll Hall
CB 3490
Chapel Hill, NC 27514-3490
(919) 962-3116

Integral unit of Frank Hawkins Kenan Institute of Private Enterprise at University of North Carolina at Chapel Hill.

Index

289